W0246926

PENGUIN VEER

KARGIL

Rachna Bisht Rawat is the author of six books published by Penguin Random House India, including the bestseller *The Brave: Param Vir Chakra Stories*. She lives in Gurugram with Hukum, the bright-eyed, bushy-tailed golden retriever; an eclectic collection of books and music; and Manoj Rawat, the man in olive green who met her when he was a gentleman cadet at the Indian Military Academy and offered to be her comrade for life. Occasionally, they are visited by Saransh the Wise, who has moved out to explore the world on his own. She can be reached at rachnabisht@gmail.com. Her Instagram handle is @ rachna_bishtrawat.

PRAISE FOR THE BOOK

'Compelling and mind-blowing stories about the heroes of the Kargil War that capture the very essence, ethos and motivation of the Indian soldier. A must-read for every Indian citizen'—Maj. Gen. Ian Cardozo, AVSM, SM (Retd)

'Kargil stories have become the stuff of legends—stories that deserve to be shared and told over and over again. Rachna Bisht Rawat takes a deep look at the human face of warfare in the high Himalayas and comes out with a moving insight of the psyche and raw courage of Indian soldiers. Rachna's account will undoubtedly make any Indian's heart swell with pride'—Rehan Fazal, BBC

'*Kargil* is not a linear account of a war that Indians saw beamed into their living rooms via television. It goes beyond the tales of sacrifice, love and remembrance that families, friends and regiments have kept alive these past twenty years. The book addresses why, in a world where these young men could have been anything, they chose the way of the warrior and the old-fashioned, rare ideals that go with it. This is something that stays with you long after the last bullet has been fired and the last page has been turned'—Deepa Alexander, senior deputy editor, *The Hindu*

'These stories take you to the frontlines. [They are not] about tact, but raw courage, determination, dedication and camaraderie. Also about soldiers' families; how they cope with tension and tragedies when their loved ones are fighting on the frontline. Only a talented army daughter and wife could have written it'—Gen. Ved Prakash Malik, former chief of Army Staff

'Rachna Bisht Rawat's *Kargil: Untold Stories from the War* deals with vignettes that involve the soldier's family and have fallen through the gaps in our memory'—*The Hindu*

'Timed to the 20th anniversary of Kargil, Rachna Bisht Rawat's book pays rich tribute to the martyrs, survivors, families, ordinary citizens and others who were affected by the war. Married to an army officer who fought in Kargil, the writer brings her lived experience and journalistic training to piece together a difficult, often harrowing story'—*Mint*

25TH ANNIVERSARY EDITION

KARGIL

UNTOLD STORIES FROM THE WAR

Rachna Bisht Rawat

VEER

An imprint of Penguin Random House

PENGUIN VEER

Penguin Veer is an imprint of the Penguin Random House group of companies
whose addresses can be found at global.penguinrandomhouse.com

Published by Penguin Random House India Pvt. Ltd
4th Floor, Capital Tower 1, MG Road,
Gurugram 122 002, Haryana, India

Penguin
Random House
India

First published in Ebury Press by Penguin Random House India 2019
Published in Penguin Veer by Penguin Random House India 2022
This revised edition published by Penguin Random House India 2024

The painting on the cover is the artist's reimagination of a scenario where all
the heroes of Kargil would have returned to us alive. It has been visualized by
designer Gunjan Ahlawat and brought to life by illustrator Amit Srivastava.

The views and opinions expressed in this book are the author's own and the
facts are as reported by her which have been verified to the extent possible,
and the publishers are not in any way liable for the same.

Please note that no part of this book may be used or reproduced in any manner
for the purpose of training artificial intelligence technologies or systems.

ISBN 9780143445845

Typeset in Adobe Garamond Pro by Manipal Digital Systems, Manipal
Printed at Gopsons Papers Pvt. Ltd., Noida

www.penguin.co.in

MIX
Paper | Supporting
responsible forestry
FSC® C191020

For the soldiers who did not return from Kargil, and their families, whose debt the country can never repay

'To live in the hearts we leave behind, is not to die'

—Thomas Campbell

In early 1999, exactly twenty years ago, Pakistani regulars, disguised as jihadis, crossed over into the cold barren heights of Kargil, and established posts in Indian territory. Their brazen infiltration triggered a sharp limited war between India and Pakistan. It was a tough war, fought on sheer grit and courage, as gutsy young officers, most of them in their twenties, led equally brave soldiers up naked rock faces and managed to evict the enemy within weeks. On 26 July 1999, the Kargil conflict officially came to an end. The Indian Army announced complete eviction of Pakistani intruders; but a price was paid for it in blood and tears. We had lost 527 of our brave soldiers; 1363 came back wounded.

Contents

Message from the Raksha Mantri

I am happy to learn that, when the nation is celebrating the twentieth anniversary of Kargil Vijay, Ms Rachna Bisht Rawat is coming out with a book narrating the untold stories from the Kargil War.

We remember India's war heroes and fallen soldiers by revisiting their stories of sacrifices. We rejoice by celebrating the victories in war and, in this process, renew our resolve to safeguard the honour of the Tricolour.

I am hopeful that this well-timed book on Kargil warriors will revisit their stories, rejoice in their victories and keep the memories of our brave soldiers alive for coming generations.

I extend my best wishes to the author and hope for its successful publication.

Rajnath Singh
New Delhi
15 July 2019

Foreword

I am the proud father of Kargil martyr Lieutenant (Lt) Vijyant Thapar (Robin), Vir Chakra (VrC), who laid down his life for his country at the age of twenty-two. Losing Robin, our young son, in the Kargil War, when he had the best years of his life ahead of him, has been a terrible personal loss for both my wife and me. It broke our hearts forever. However, it is also the greatest honour of our lives. Besides being Robin's father, I am also an Army officer and I believe dying in battle for the country is a privilege. It is what all of us in uniform dream about, but very few get the opportunity. Our son was a fortunate man indeed.

When death comes is inconsequential, as come it must. What really matters is how and where it comes. Life is never measured in terms of its length but in terms of its depth or the intensity with which it is lived. What Robin and the other martyrs of Kargil achieved in their twenties was far greater than what many long insipid lives did. All of us who lost their children in this war, and the wars before, are so proud of them. I am sure the same applies to the young wives who lost their husbands and children who lost their fathers. We live with the loss and the pain, but we also live with our heads held high. We believe these men we loved so much shall continue to live—till we remember their sacrifice. The onus of keeping them alive rests on us, the ones left behind. The nation has the responsibility to remember them with reverence because that was the trust with which they fell. We must ensure that their stories are passed down the generations. *Kargil: Untold Stories from the War* is a great effort in that direction.

Every book is a monument; it enshrines an event, a person or a thought. This book immortalizes the spirit of the officers and soldiers of the Indian Army who made the Kargil War an expression of dedication to duty, indomitable spirit, bravery and sacrifice. It is a testimony to the courage, grit and determination of the young men to get on the objective, despite death staring them in the face. The stories epitomize all that makes the Indian Army great. It also chronicles the graceful and dignified acceptance of their loss and pain, by mothers and wives who lost their sons and husbands.

Whenever the story of Kargil is told, it shall be incomplete without paying homage to the steely resolve and cold courage of these young men who went to fight for their nation knowing that they might never return.

Barely out of the academy, they fought against all odds, with single-minded devotion, and set new benchmarks in heroism. Their spirit and daring will be difficult to replicate.

Every young officer in every new batch that graduates from the Indian Military Academy (IMA) and the Officers Training Academy (OTA) takes the 'Antim Pag' only after taking the oath: I will observe and obey all the commands of the President of the Union of India and the commands of any officer set above me, even to the peril of my life. They have proved true to this oath time and again. Alongside they have their regimental pride to uphold.

A victory in war is achieved because battles are won. Battles are won when soldiers put duty before themselves. This book pays tribute to this do-or-die spirit of the Indian armed forces. Soldiers who put their lives at stake in wars and war-like situations expect nothing in return. But what the nation owes to them is recognition and gratitude. Documenting the sagas of their sacrifices is a part of this process. These tales need to be part of not just military history but also school textbooks, so that every generation of our country is reminded of the sacrifices made by its soldiers and young people are motivated to emulate the same.

I am sure that the stories written by Mrs Rachna Bisht Rawat, who writes from her heart, will continue to inspire future generations of soldiers and motivate them to follow the footsteps of the brave young heroes who won the Kargil War for us.

I take this opportunity to recognize the contribution of every single soldier of the Indian Army who fought for our country and shall continue to do so. I salute their sacrifice and selfless devotion to duty. I take great pride in having been a part of an army of such exemplary men. It is indeed an honour that I, my son, my father and his father before him have served this splendid organization where we give our all and ask for nothing in return.

Jai Hind!

Col. V.N. Thapar (Retd)

Introduction

With the exception of my young readers, who are not yet twenty, all of us have lived through the Kargil War. Some of us saw it unfolding on our television screens while others had a closer look. I was a reporter with the *Indian Express*, Ahmedabad, newly married to Captain (Capt.) Manoj Rawat of 3 Engineer Regiment when the war broke out. My husband's unit was among those immediately deployed on the Rajasthan border because of a perceived threat.

Even as I watched the goings-on of war with a sinking heart, the entire cantonment was emptied of men and machines within a few days. Noisy messes, where ice cubes clinked in crystal glasses, were suddenly quiet; the stomp of DMS boots was not heard in parade grounds any more; parks no longer rang out with the laughter of dads throwing balls to little children with poised bats. I would stand in my balcony and watch convoys of Army trucks head for the border carrying soldiers in combat greens, rifles slung across their backs, faces sombre. My handsome husband bid goodbye with a curt handshake, since an officer will not be seen hugging his wife in front of his troops. He did smile at me lovingly from the driver's seat and, with a crisp salute, told me to take care, that he would be back soon. He then drove off, his jeep disappearing in a cloud of dust. The solace of my life is that he did return. So many husbands never did.

The war was eventually restricted to Kargil. My twenty-five-year-old brother, then Capt. Sameer Singh Bisht, fought it alongside his unit, 5 Para. Those were terrible days indeed. I would scan every newspaper, watch every news channel, stay awake in my bed with Sufi, the cat, and wait for dawn to break. In the morning, I would go to work and beg, borrow, steal any war-related assignments I could from my editor, Derick D'Sa. Accompanied by a photographer, I would travel to villages where the bodies of martyrs were being brought home. I would cover funerals, join processions and watch grieving families and little children whose lives would never be the same again. I would think of the men in my life who were at risk too and my heart would sink. Late evenings, returning from office, I would park my bright blue scooter at an STD (subscriber trunk dialing) booth and call home in Kotdwar, a small town in Garhwal (Uttarakhand), where my parents lived in a mango tree-surrounded bungalow ever since my paratrooper father, Brigadier (Brig.) B.S. Bisht, Sena

Medal (SM), Vishisht Seva Medal (VSM), had retired. It was always Mom who picked up the phone.

Dad, she said, was glued to the television watching war bulletins, trying to figure out where my brother could be. He had almost stopped eating and would sit silently in the veranda late at night with the light switched off; his head held high, a cigarette dangling from between his fingers, a glass of whiskey by his side and Farida Khanum's voice wafting out of our sitting room window from the old cassette player inside. His suffering ended when his son returned from Kargil a decorated officer. He was lucky. There were many whose sons never did.

In the course of writing *Kargil*, I met some of these fathers—and mothers. And children with hazy memories of that man called father, a stranger in olive green, who had left home one day and never come back. When I asked Kargil martyr Lance Naik Bachan Singh's son, Lt Hitesh, to share some memories of his father, he said he hardly had any. 'My twin brother and I were four when he died, but I do remember his funeral,' he told me. Mrs Kamesh Bala, Hitesh's mother, told me that in the seven years of being married she had spent just five months with her husband. He had promised to take her and the twins along in the peace posting he was expecting, but that day never came. Bachan died at twenty-nine in the Battle of Tololing.

Capt. Saurabh Kalia was twenty-two when he signed the first cheque of his life soon after being commissioned and handed it to his mother proudly, telling her, 'Don't worry about money any more, *ab main kamane laga hun* [I am earning now].' Mrs Kalia showed me the cancelled cheque with tears in her eyes. It was never cashed. Saurabh was dead before his first salary was credited to his bank account.

Mrs Meena Nayyar told me how the pampered Anuj would keep pestering her and her husband for a new car that he wanted them to buy for him before he got back. 'I would get exasperated each time the phone rang. We didn't think he would never return,' she said. Anuj was to get married to his school sweetheart in September 1999. In July, he was dead.

I met Capt. Haneef-ud-din's mother, Mrs Hema Aziz. Haneef's body lay on the frozen snow in Turtuk for forty-three days. When the then Army Chief, General (Gen.) Ved Prakash Malik, visited Mrs Aziz and told her that they were not able to retrieve his body because the enemy was firing constantly, she assured him that she did not want another soldier to risk his life to get her son's body. She even refused the petrol pump that was offered to her on Haneef's martyrdom.

I am sure there are heartbreaking stories like this on the other side of the border too. I marvel at how men who are fathers, sons, brothers, husbands and lovers just lace up their boots and go to war, honouring their sole responsibility as soldiers. War stories might sound romantic, but the reality is that war is terrible. It destroys lives, shatters families and leaves behind a legacy of sadness and hate. I sincerely hope that the martyrs of Kargil are the last ones we have to grieve. This book is a tribute to their courage and, even more so, to the courage of their families, who have faced their loss with such dignity. We are under their debt—a debt that can never be repaid.

In his last letter to his father, Lt Vijyant Thapar had hoped that the sacrifices of his men would not be forgotten. This book is a step in that direction. I hope that *Kargil: Untold Stories from the War* shall keep the memories of these brave soldiers alive in public memory. That is the least we can do for those who willingly gave up their lives for the country. Soldiers don't die on battlefields; they die when an ungrateful nation forgets their sacrifice. May the 527 martyrs of Kargil live in our hearts forever.

Chapter 1

Unbroken

A young officer is tortured to death in enemy custody. His father vows to get the guilty punished.

14 May 1999
2.30 p.m.
Somewhere near Bajrang Post, Kaksar, Kargil

It has been more than four hours of walking in the chilling wind. The cold is seeping into twenty-two-year-old Capt. Saurabh Kalia's bones. Most of the climb from 99 Top, where he received orders to take a surveillance patrol to Bajrang Post, has been along a frozen nullah. He knows the nullah is deceptive. There is ice on top but biting-cold water flows underneath. One wrong step and a man could fall in and freeze to death.

1

The chill in the air is making his eyes water. He uses the back of his hand to wipe them dry. The air seems to be freezing on his eyelashes; he runs his tongue over dry chapped lips. A Himachali, he is used to the cold but the temperature is unbearable even for him.

For a moment, he stops and his thoughts wander to Palampur's brilliant blue skies and jade-green tea gardens. And home. He thinks about his parents and Vaibhav, his happy-go-lucky younger brother who is still in college, and it suffuses his heart with warmth. He wonders how his five soldiers are faring. Turning his head slightly to look back, he finds them plodding on tenaciously.

Pulling his balaclava lower over his ears, Saurabh shakes his fingers to get the blood flowing again and starts walking. His carbine hangs behind his back. Up ahead, he can see Bajrang Post. Located at 17,450 feet on the southwestern flank of Kaksar, it overlooks the vast, open glaciated area but has been vacated by the Indian Army for the winter months, when it lies buried under heavy snow. As per a long-standing agreement between India and Pakistan, both sides vacate these posts during winter and reoccupy them in summer. Saurabh has been sent to check if the snow has melted enough for the post to be manned again. He has no intention of returning before he completes his task.

Gritting his teeth, he moves on, unaware that the enemy is watching him. Taking advantage of India's trust, Pakistan has slowly been moving its troops into Bajrang Post during the past few months. Even as the unsuspecting soldiers of 4 JAT climb to what they think is their own vacant post, they are being watched by the enemy who is waiting for them to come within firing distance. At 2.30 p.m., Saurabh loses radio contact with his men from Charlie Company at 99 Top.

———

21 December 2018
Gaggal airport
Kangra, Himachal Pradesh

On a cold December morning, when the temperature has dipped to 5 degrees, a tiny ATR-72 aircraft taxies down the runway and comes to a smooth stop. Wrapping mufflers tighter around their necks and slipping into warm jackets, the passengers pull their cabin baggage down from overhead storage compartments and queue up to alight. Mesmerized by the stunning view that accosts them, most stop to take selfies with the twin-engine plane and the magnificent snow-covered Dhauladhar range as a backdrop.

Walking across the tarmac to one of the smallest airports I have seen, I don't share my co-passengers' euphoria though the view and the fragrant roses blooming outside do take my breath away. I am taking a taxi to Palampur to meet Dr Narinder K. Kalia, the seventy-year-old father of late Capt. Saurabh Kalia who, along with his five comrades, was captured by Pakistan in 1999. The men were tortured for more than three weeks and their bodies returned to India after they were shot through the head. I have read the post-mortem reports and they have kept me awake many nights. What was done to Saurabh and his men is beyond human imagination. I too have a son and I shudder to imagine the lifetime of pain that has befallen Saurabh's parents. Dr Kalia has written to every important government department, every prime minister, every embassy and consulate he could find the addresses of to take up this case of human rights violations and flouting of the Geneva Conventions by Pakistan, but nothing has come of it so far.

Meeting Dr Kalia is my personal effort to walk a small distance with him in his long and relentless fight for justice. It is also an effort to absolve myself of some of the guilt that comes from being the citizen of a country that could not stand by its soldiers. But right now I am preoccupied with other thoughts. Like, how do you start a conversation with a father whose young son faced the most horrific end? Is there anything one can say to take away some of his pain? How did a simple middle-class man from a small hill town, who retired as a senior scientist from the Council of Scientific and Industrial Research, who stutters when he talks and struggles to form the words he wants to say, find the courage to take on the government of his country? How has he managed to fight with the same passion for nineteen long years, with hardly any small victories on the way? I find no answers to my own questions and, switching off my mind, look out of the window instead.

Around me are breathtaking mountains that chill the air and send it fresh and crisp straight into my lungs. Beside me, the winding blue-green Neugal Khud meanders lazily through Palampur.

This is where Saurabh Kalia—Naughty, as his parents called him—grew up and went to school, first to DAV Public School and then to Kendriya Vidyalaya in the cantonment, where he watched, with long-lashed luminous eyes, the splendours of life in uniform. This is where the little boy was seduced by the discipline, smart uniforms, the romance of putting your life at stake for your country and decided he wanted to be an Army officer too.

In the small hill town of Palampur, you don't need addresses to reach the houses of martyrs (the late Capt. Vikram Batra, Param Vir Chakra (PVC), was from here too and I had the same experience when I came looking for his house five years ago while researching my book *The Brave*). This time I am wiser—I haven't insisted that Dr Kalia send me his complete address as I had done with Mr Girdhari Lal Batra, Vikram's father, when he had said, '*Beta, Palampur mein kisi se bhi puch lena, humare ghar ka rasta bata denge.* [Ask anyone in Palampur, they will direct you to our house.]'

All I do now is put my head out of the window and ask, '*Kya aapko Capt. Saurabh Kalia ka ghar maloom hai?*' [Do you know Capt. Saurabh Kalia's house?]' People smile and nod. Women with shawls draped over their heads,

a bespectacled tailor oiling his sewing machine, an old
man smoking a surreptitious bidi, and effervescent salwar
kameez-clad schoolgirls with pink cheeks and ribbons in
their braids guide me with gestures of the hand and tilts
of the head.

Crossing tea gardens strewn along the roadside like
emeralds in a necklace, we weave our way past houses with
bright red and green roofs. Vipin Ji (my taxi driver) and I
don't bother with road signs or Google Maps; we follow
directions that lead us in no time to a house with a sign
at the gate that tells us we have reached a family that has
borne personal loss. It is the internationally recognized
icon of an upside-down rifle with a war helmet placed on
top— a tribute to fallen soldiers. The dates 29 June 1976
to 9 June 1999, inscribed on black marble beneath Capt.
Saurabh Kalia's name, are a reminder that he died before
the best years of his life, before he could dream and stretch
out an arm to reach for whatever he wanted. He chose to
be a soldier but he could be one only for six months. His
lone nameplate at the gate tells me that he continues to
live here, if only in the hearts of his parents and his brother
who never felt the need to have their own names there.

Dr Kalia greets me with a smile. Mrs Vijaya Kalia,
Saurabh's mother, pushes aside my folded hands and
envelopes me in such a long hug that all my professional
apprehensions and personal sadness melt away. My eyes fill
with tears at how much she has lost and how much she is
still capable of giving.

We cross a room that has Saurabh Smriti Kaksh written outside. 'We will bring you here later. First you must have breakfast,' Dr Kalia tells me, escorting me up to the terrace where a glass hut protects us from the chilly wind but allows us to soak in the sun and the surreal view of the snow-clad mountains.

I spend the entire day with the Kalias, with Vaibhav, their younger son, joining us, and my guilt slowly dissipates in the warmth of their affection. They tell me how Naughty was as a boy—quiet and reticent, fond of cooking for his family and friends. They joke about how difficult it was to wake him up in the mornings and how when Mrs Kalia was told that in the IMA early risers were ordered to wear boots and run on top of late risers, she quickly got Saurabh an alarm clock, telling him worriedly, '*Tu toh subah uthta hi nahi hai beta; tere upar toh woh roz boot waale ladke daudayenge*. [You can never wake up early, son; they will make boys with boots run on top of you every day.]'

Vaibhav doubles up laughing when he tells me that when Saurabh came back on his first term break from the academy, he had lost so much weight that his friends joked, '*Faujiyon ne toh alu chheel diya*! [The Army seems to have peeled our potato!]' He also tells me that Saurabh wanted to be a doctor earlier but he was captivated by the charms of the Army cantonment when he started going to school there. '*Unka kya discipline hai, hum logon se ekdum alag. Main bhi sochta hun Army mein chala jaun*. [What fantastic discipline they have; they are so different from us. I also think I will join the Army]', he would tell Vaibhav when the brothers were together.

Saurabh had given his medical entrance exams but could not get into a good college. He knew his parents would find it difficult to afford a capitation fee. Mrs Kalia says that she had told him that if he really wanted to be a doctor, they would manage the money somehow; but Saurabh had looked at her with a disdainful smile and walked out of the room saying, '*Mujhe thappe wallah doctor nahin ban na*. [I don't want to be a doctor with a fake stamp.]'

After graduating from C.S.K. Himachal Pradesh Agriculture University, Palampur, Saurabh had cleared his Combined Defence Services (CDS) exam and joined the IMA in August 1997. Both his parents had gone for his passing out parade on 12 December 1998 after which he had come home on a short break. Delighted that he would now start getting a salary, he had given a blank signed cheque to his mother, telling her magnanimously, 'I have started earning. You don't have to worry about money any more. '*Jab zarurat ho nikal lena*. [You can withdraw money whenever you need it].' Ironically, neither he nor his mother withdrew any money from his bank. When his first salary was credited, Saurabh was dead.

After spending about fifteen days with his family, Saurabh had taken the train to Bareilly where he had to report to the Jat Regimental Centre on 29 December, before joining his battalion, 4 Jat, in Kashmir. Proud that he was joining one of the longest-serving and most decorated regiments of the Indian Army, he had waved goodbye to his parents as the train started moving and had stretched out an arm as if to touch his mother's feet. '*Maa, tum dekhna ek din aisa kaam kar jaunga ki saari duniya mein mera naam hoga* [Mother, just you wait, one day you will be proud of me],' he had said. She had laughed and replied, '*Bada aaya naam kamane waala. Tu theek se Bareilly pahunch ja bas utna hi kaafi hai.*' [Really! If you reach Bareilly safe, that should be enough for me].'

There had been a few letters from him after that, one after his dining in, telling his parents that in his first speech in the officers mess he had shyly told his unit, 'Today, I am proud to be in 4 Jat. One day 4 Jat shall be proud of me.' He had called home on 30 April 1999 to wish Vaibhav on his twentieth birthday. He had said he was going ahead to the forward posts and might not be able to stay in touch for a while. 'Don't worry about me if I don't call or write. I shall be home for my birthday (29 June),' he had said. And then there had been silence. Saurabh Kalia was never to call the family he loved so much again.

In the first week of June, Vaibhav was shocked to come across an *Indian Express* report saying Radio Pakistan in Skardu had reported the capture of an Indian Army officer. Without saying anything to his mother, he had gone across to his father's office and they had both visited Holta Cantonment. They were horrified to learn that Saurabh had been missing since early May. On 9 June at 7.30 p.m., Pakistan returned six mauled and disfigured bodies to India. The dead were identified as Capt. Saurabh Kalia, and Riflemen Arjun Ram Baswana, Mula Ram Bidiasar, Naresh Singh Sinsinwar, Bhanwar Lal Bagaria and Bhika Ram Mudh of 4 Jat. Saurabh had been twenty-two, Arjun Ram just eighteen.

It was later revealed that Capt. Saurabh Kalia and his men were kept in captivity from 15 May 1999 to 7 June 1999 (over twenty-two days), and were subjected to torture as became evident from the injuries to their bodies. Post-mortem examinations revealed that the soldiers had been tortured with burning cigarettes, piercing eardrums with hot rods, puncturing eyes before removing them, breaking most of their teeth and bones, fracturing their skulls, and cutting off lips, noses and private organs. They had finally been shot dead, as evidenced by bullet wounds to the temple. The post-mortems also confirmed that the injuries were inflicted ante-mortem (before death).

Then Army Chief Gen V.P. Malik says in his book *Kargil—From Surprise to Victory* that the Army had requested the International Committee of the Red Cross and the Indian Red Cross to carry out the post-mortems but both agencies declined. Ultimately, the post mortems had to be done by the Army Hospital, Delhi Cantonment, and torture was confirmed. A shocked and visibly upset external affairs minister Jaswant Singh, a former soldier himself, had briefed the media personally after seeing the reports and had called it a civilizational crime against all humanity, a reversion to barbaric medievalism.

Vaibhav says he went to the cantonment when Saurabh's body was finally brought to Palampur. 'They showed me his face to reconfirm his identity. It was in a shocking state, there was almost nothing on it except his eyebrows. I told my parents not to look.'

Saurabh was cremated in Palampur, the beautiful land of blooming roses, sparkling water and snow-capped Dhauladhars, where he had grown up and spent the happiest years of his life. Mrs Vijaya Kalia, who suffered a heart attack the day she heard Saurabh had gone missing, gave up her government job soon after his death but says she did not shed a single tear for him. 'It would have diluted the magnitude of his sacrifice. I am very proud of my son. He gave his life for his country.'

A shattered Dr Kalia vowed that he would fight for the human rights of his son and five comrades who were subjected to torture for more than three weeks and make sure that the guilty were punished. 'In those days in captivity, they fought the Kargil War, alone and unarmed,' he says.

Dr Kalia's journey has been long and painful with roadblocks at every stage. 'Saurabh was a soldier. He was doing his duty. For parents to know that their son gave his life for his country is a matter of great pride. But to know that he was so brutally tortured in enemy custody is something that no parent, no Army and no country should tolerate,' he says. 'It doesn't matter whether I get any success or not. I shall continue to fight for these soldiers till I die.' The quiet dignity on his face stays with me for days.

Over the years, visitors to Palampur have continued to walk into the Kalias' home, offering condolences for what their son had to undergo. Letters of support have been brought to them from the Palampur post office in sacks. Dr Kalia's mailbox continues to receive emails of support. There are more than two lakh signatures on a public petition for justice filed by Dr Kalia. A young artist has visited with a beautiful painting of Saurabh, his young face looking out from inside the fluttering Tricolour; a scientist from European Organization for Nuclear Research (CERN), who had come for a lecture to Hamirpur, travelled to meet the Kalias and implored them to come and live with her in Switzerland, offering to buy tickets for them. One of the most touching tributes came from a Pakistani settled in the US, who sent Dr Kalia a copy of the Quran and some seeds of flowering plants. 'I am very sorry for what happened to Saurabh,' he wrote, with deep regret. 'Our country is now controlled by mullahs.'

Before leaving, I take off my shoes and take a round of Saurabh Smriti Kaksh that Saurabh's parents have put together with so much affection. The room holds the few photographs the Kalias have of him in uniform, his black tin trunk, his uniforms, his voter ID card, six pairs of shoes that he owned, a bottle of Chelpark ink, an alarm clock with his name on it, a Park Avenue aftershave lotion, the wallet that was recovered from his body, a poster of Aishwarya Rai that he had put up in his room at the IMA and a photograph of late Capt. Amit Bhardwaj, of 4 Jat, who led a patrol to search for Saurabh a day after he went missing. The patrol had come under devastating enemy fire and Capt. Bhardwaj had been martyred near the same post, along with two other soldiers. His body could not be recovered for fifty-seven days. My heart is heavy when I take the flight back to Delhi.

Typing out the story on my laptop in my blower-warmed study a week later, I go through my cell phone's photo gallery. I spend many minutes looking at a picture I took of Dr Kalia standing beside Saurabh's garlanded portrait in uniform. There is an uncanny resemblance between the father and son. They share the same bone structure, the same lips and nose, there is the same quiet resolve in their eyes, and they even wear similar moustaches. I look at another picture I have taken from their family album. A younger Dr Kalia is laughing with an arm around Saurabh, who must have been in college then. I wonder if he has ever laughed like that again. Another picture has Saurabh in a thick sweater, shyly hugging his mother. They are both smiling into the camera.

While Saurabh remains twenty-two forever, in photographs, in memories and in conversations, the Kalias have aged considerably. Mrs Kalia has a heart condition and walks slowly on arthritis-afflicted legs. Dr Kalia's hair is almost grey. They both smile but the shadow of a heartbreaking sadness lurks constantly on their faces. I sincerely hope that one day, there will be justice for Saurabh, and some of that pain will go.

Author's Note

In spite of incriminating evidence, and then external affairs minister Jaswant Singh's initial outrage, the Indian government did not move the International Court of Justice (ICJ) against the treatment meted out to the six soldiers stating that it did not have jurisdiction over Indian and Pakistani matters that needed to be sorted out bilaterally as per the Shimla Agreement.

Dr Kalia continues to fight a case in the Supreme Court to pressure the central government to demand an international probe. Those in diplomatic circles say that Pakistan had moved the ICJ immediately after the Kargil conflict when the Indian Air Force (IAF) had shot down a Pakistan Navy Atlantique aircraft in Gujarat. However, India had then cited a 1974 declaration that ruled out the jurisdiction of the ICJ over cases involving present or past Commonwealth Nations. If India approaches the ICJ with the Kalia case, Pakistan is likely to use the same provisions to block the move. Alternatively, if the Indian government does approach the ICJ, the safeguard will become invalid and open India up to international arbitration on issues such as Jammu and Kashmir (J&K). Pakistan will then have the option of approaching the ICJ in the future if it wants to rake up any issues against India, such as human rights violations in Kashmir.

However, India has approached the ICJ in the Kulbhushan Jadhav case. Jadhav was sentenced to death by a Pakistani military court on charges of espionage and terrorism in April 2017. A ten-member ICJ bench on 18 May 2017 restrained Pakistan from executing Jadhav till the case was adjudicated on. This has given new hope to the Kalias.

This chapter is based on conversations with the Kalia family and their advocate in the Supreme Court, Arvind Sharma, who holds copies of the post-mortem reports. Saurabh's last patrol description has been recreated from an interview with Naib Subedar Pinku Kumar, one of the survivors from late Capt. Amit Bhardwaj's patrol that had gone looking for Saurabh.

Chapter 2

Not without My Men

A Ladakhi Buddhist officer climbs a glacier to reach his men who have been pinned down by the enemy and are fast running out of ammunition.

30 May 1999
10.30 a.m.
BSF Base Camp
Handangbrok, Batalik

The AN/PRC-25 (Army Navy/Portable Radio Communication) radio set is buzzing for the third time this morning. Sonam, who is having a steaming hot mug of langar chai, puts it down and responds.

'*Sahab, dushman ka fire aur tez ho gaya hai. Aap nahi aaye toh hum zinda nahi bachenge* [Sir, enemy fire has intensified. If you don't come, we will all die].'

There is so much disturbance on the radio set that Sonam cannot recognize which of his men is speaking, but he can hear the panic in the voice. To him, it sounds like his comrade of many daring missions, Havaldar (Hav.) Sonam Rigzin, one of the bravest soldiers he has known.

'*Chinta mat karo, main aa raha hun* [Don't worry, I am coming],' Sonam says, his voice steely. Picking up the static line, he asks to be connected to the Subsector Commander at Dah.

'Sir, my boys are in grave danger. I need to go to them,' he says.

'I'm sorry, Sonam, the Brigade Commander is busy in briefings. You will have to wait for orders,' the officer replies, expressing his helplessness.

Broad-shouldered, tanned and finely muscled, with a physique built not at a gym but by climbing mountains in the course of duty, Sonam gets up and goes looking for his Commanding Officer (CO). Though Colonel (Col.) A.S. Chandoke has not been in the chain of command since the Kargil War started, and Sonam's company is on a mission directly under 70 Infantry Brigade, he is visiting to see how his men are faring.

'Sir, it has been an hour and a half since my boys have been asking for help,' Sonam says. 'If their ammunition runs out, they will either be killed or captured. If anything happens to them, I will never be able to forgive myself. Please let me go.'

'OK, Sonam,' Col. Chandoke replies, his brow furrowed, 'Go! I'll take responsibility for you.'

———

October 2018
Beverly Park Apartments
Dwarka, Delhi

The bell rings just once. Though I take a while to open the door, outside there is unhurried calm. Col. Sonam Wangchuk, Maha Vir Chakra (MVC), waits patiently with a gentle smile on his face, radiating a monk-like tranquillity.

There is so much that I have read and heard about the legendary Buddhist warrior that seeing him in my house feels a little surreal. He has driven down from Khel Gaon, where he is staying on his visit to see his son, who studies in Delhi.

It has been nineteen years since the Kargil War. Col. Wangchuk retired from the Army earlier this year and now helps out with the administration of a vipassana centre in Leh, where he is a trustee. He shakes hands with my pleased husband, compliments him on his physique and backslaps our son, Saransh, who is just back from school and has dumped his bag to rush to the sitting room to see what the Kargil hero looks like in real life. Within minutes Col. Wangchuk has our golden retriever sprawled at his feet and the three of us sitting around him, completely captivated. Leaning back on our old red sofa, a cup of coffee in hand, Col. Wangchuk tells us his amazing story of grit and courage.

Strangely enough, this war story begins with the Dalai Lama.

———

25 May 1999
His Holiness the Dalai Lama's residence
Jivetsal, Choglamsar

It is a beautiful summer morning in Ladakh. The sky is the deep cerulean blue of impressionistic paintings, the air is crystal clear and the sun seems to be smiling at the colourful prayer flags fluttering in the breeze. It is hard to imagine that not too far away, dark, brooding war clouds are looming.

Clad in maroon robes, a gentle smile on his face, the Dalai Lama stands on the porch, arms outstretched in blessing. He is facing a large contingent of Ladakhi soldiers in uniform. Bareheaded and unarmed, they step up to him one by one, heads bowed in reverence. His Holiness reaches out to hold their faces in his hands; he places a srunga (sacred thread) around each one's neck. The lamas standing with him hand out small packets of chinglap (small balls of prasad). Both signify the Dalai Lama's blessings and are an assurance to the soldiers that they carry his protection to the battlefield.

In the age group of twenty-five to thirty-five, the men are accompanied by their Company Commander, Major (Maj.) Sonam Wangchuk. They have come from Karu, 25 km away, and will soon be on their way to Batalik to join the war with Pakistan. All the men are Buddhists but this is their time to do their duty as soldiers of the Ladakh Scouts, a border-guarding force that functions directly under the Defence Ministry. Maj. Sonam has joined them from 4 Assam Rifles; he is on deputation from the Indian Army.

Meeting over, the men sprint back to the parking area. Their trucks wind their way back to Karu. Sonam, sitting in front with the driver, rests against the seat. Hearing the soldiers talking in the back of the vehicle, he can sense their lifted spirits. Assured that his men are now mentally ready for battle, he silently mouths the prayer 'Ki ki so so, lhar gyalo', meaning victory to the gods.

That morning with the Dalai Lama was very crucial, Col. Wangchuk tells us. 'When we received orders to join the war, it was not clear who the intruders were. We had heard they were not regular soldiers of the Pakistani Army but mujahedeen. The langar gossip was that the men manning those heights were brutal, cruel and inhuman. *Seedhe aankhon ke beech mein goli maar dete hain* [They shoot to kill]. The morale of our young soldiers had plummeted. They were apprehensive about going to fight an enemy they knew nothing about.'

Col. Wangchuk says this was conveyed to him by senior Junior Commissioned Officer (JCO) Subedar Tsering Stobdan, VrC. '*Yeh log toh pehle se hi haar maan ke baithe huye hain. Kuch karna padega, Sahab* [These fellows have given up before even starting. We'll have to do something],' Tsering Sahab had told him. '*Dalai Lama aaye huye hain, agar unke darshan karwa sakte hain toh karwa dijiye* [The Dalai Lama is here. A meeting with him could lift their spirits].'

When Col. Wangchuk requested His Holiness to bless the soldiers going to war, he immediately agreed.

'We call the Dalai Lama Chandrazig, god of compassion. His blessings, the chinglap and the holy thread he'd given made us feel that he was with us. I don't think anyone ate the prasad; all of us kept it in our pockets. It was an assurance that he would protect us on the battlefield,' he explains.

———

26 May 1999
6 a.m.
Karu
To the battlefield

An Army Aviation Cheetah helicopter carries Sonam from Karu to Dah, a distance of 165 km by road. His troops climb into Shaktiman trucks and start around the same time. While Sonam reaches Dah in half an hour, the soldiers take seven hours to travel 150 km and reach Achinathang, 15 km short of Dah, where they set up camp. After two days at Dah, Sonam is told to report at the operational base camp at Handangbrok, the last post before the Line of Control (LoC) in the Chorbat La subsector of Batalik.

On May 28, Sonam collects his troops from Achinathang. His rocket launcher and medium machine gun (MMG) detachments are taken away for other operations, and so are some of his soldiers, who will be used as guides by new units who are not familiar with the terrain.

He starts for the base camp at Handangbrok, at a height of 14,000 feet, with a strength of forty soldiers and JCOs. Maj. B.S. Katoch, Second in Command (2IC), Indus Wing, Ladakh Scouts, is not there but he briefs Sonam over the static line. He tells him that, according to some reports received, the Pakistanis have been concentrating in large numbers (nearly a brigade strength of 2,000) on the LoC. They are suspected of trying to come in through Chorbat La. Sonam is asked to take a surveillance and domination patrol of one JCO and ten Other Ranks to Area Rock Fall on the LoC and verify these reports. The patrol's task is to stay there, observe and report back on a daily basis. Sonam is told to settle his patrol and then return to Handangbrok.

29 May
5 a.m.
On the glacier

Sonam and his team of Naib Subedar Tondup Dorje and
fifteen others trek down to the roadhead. They have with
them three mules carting tents, ammunition and rations.
The soldiers cross into the valley and start climbing the
glacier that looms right ahead. Since they don't have
special insulated white clothing that blends into the snowy
terrain, all of them have put on their warmest clothes—
thick brown Bhalu jackets, woollen khaki trousers and
rubber insulated snow boots. They wear thick balaclavas
on their heads and thermal inners to protect themselves
from the icy wind that stings the eyes and makes their
noses run. Heads down, the soldiers plod through the
snow for more than five hours, covering a distance of 8
km. By 10 a.m., they reach Area Rock Fall, at a height
of 18,000 feet. The air is thinner, the temperatures have
fallen further and the men can feel the cold settling into
their bones. They set up camp here. Tents are erected
quickly and a stove fixed so that rejuvenating hot tea can
be made.

Sonam takes two soldiers with him and climbs the
ridge in front, trying to find out if there are any Pakistani
soldiers on the other side.

'Everything seemed peaceful so I assumed the reports
of enemy build up were incorrect,' he says.

Relieved, he spends the afternoon with his men. Around 4.30 p.m., he returns to camp with five of the soldiers, leaving instructions with Dorje Sahab to climb up the hill at first light every morning, keep the Pakistani side under observation through the day, and climb down in the evening. He has absolutely no idea that the enemy is actually around on the vast ridgeline and that the situation will change overnight.

The very next morning he gets a phone call from his team of eleven men saying they are pinned under enemy fire and fast running out of ammunition.

———

30 May 1999
12 p.m.
Operation Rock Fall

Within an hour of getting permission from his CO, Sonam is out of the camp. He has with him three JCOs and twenty-five Other Ranks, fully armed, and also an MMG detachment from another unit. The soldiers walk down to the roadhead and cross over to the glacier, carrying on their backs 30 kg haversacks weighed down with ammunition, winter jackets, sleeping bags, socks, sweaters, food etc.

Talking to me nineteen years later, Col. Wangchuk says he almost ran through the knee-deep snow. 'There was only one thought on my mind. If something happens to my men, log kya kehenge? Company Commander aaram se baitha raha, uske sipahi maare gaye [People would have said, the Company Commander ensured his safety while his men were slaughtered]. I couldn't have lived with that shame.'

The Ladakhis could keep up with him but the non-Ladakhi component of the team—soldiers who formed the MMG detachment—were not used to the glaciated terrain and slow down, delaying the main body. 'In two hours I had reached the mouth of the U-shaped ridge with the LoC on my left, where the Pakistanis were sitting. When I stopped to count the men with me, there were just four. The rest were trailing almost 800 metres behind,' Col. Wangchuk remembers.

Sonam decides to carry on, hoping the rest will catch up soon. When he is about 700 metres short of where he had left his own team, he hears enemy fire. Soon the snow around Sonam and his men starts flying, which means the shots are close enough to kill. Sonam orders his men to drop to the ground and take cover when a scream rents the air.

Hav. Tsewang Rigzin has taken a direct burst on his heart. As the others watch in horror, a deep red stain spreads on the snow under the fallen soldier. They crawl towards him and slip a groundsheet under him but he is losing blood fast.

'He kept saying, "*Sahab, bahut thand lag rahi hai* [Sir, I'm feeling very cold]." There was nothing we could do except wrap him in a blanket,' Col. Wangchuk recounts, his voice heavy with regret. He says the fire coming at them was so intense that he ordered his men to stop returning it and concentrate on hiding instead. 'The enemy was at a height and out of range of our INSAS rifles. There was no point in wasting ammunition.

Hav. Rigzin stays alive for half an hour. With tears in their eyes, his helpless comrades watch him die, while keeping their own heads down to avoid getting hit.

Then, just as suddenly as it had started, the fire stops. By then, Rigzin is gone. The soldiers shut his eyes and wrap him in a blanket. When the fire does not resume, Sonam and Hav. Nawang Rigdol—popularly called Hav. Number Gyareh [Number Eleven] as per the Scouts tradition of identifying a soldier by the last two digits of his army number if his name is difficult to remember—decide to go further. They leave one man behind with the martyred soldier while another is sent down to find the team trailing behind and direct them to take a different route so that they come up behind the enemy soldiers.

Sonam and Hav. Number Gyareh move on, wondering why the enemy has stopped firing.

They learn later that the Pakistanis had also run out of ammunition and were lugging it from down below, which gave Sonam time to reach his stranded patrol. 'Just as I had feared, the patrol had run out of ammunition and my men were hiding from enemy fire to save their lives,' Col. Wangchuk recounts.

A relieved Dorje Sahab tells him that early morning, when he and Hav. Sonam Rigzin, along with two men carrying a light machine gun (LMG), had climbed up to watch the Pakistan side of the LoC, they had received a big shock. Peering down they had found a steep drop where, in the weak orange glow of the morning sun, they could discern four Pakistani soldiers climbing up. They were wearing Koflach boots with spikes to get a firm foothold in the snow. Each was holding two pickaxes, one in each hand, which they were using to pull themselves up over the treacherous wall of ice.

Dorje shot down the first two while the two behind slipped down and ran away. For some time there was quiet on the enemy side but then the Pakistanis made an attempt to retrieve the bodies of the two dead soldiers. Dorje managed to shoot down one more enemy soldier. Meanwhile, the enemy post on the ridge located the Indian patrol camping on the foothill and targeted them with continuous fire, pinning them down till they ran out of ammunition. Had Sonam not come to their rescue, they would have all been killed or captured.

———

10.30 p.m.

A bright white moon hangs in the sky, lighting up the snow-clad mountains in an eerie glow. Sonam makes two attempts to climb the ridge but is sent backtracking each time by a volley of enemy fire. He realizes that he and his men are under enemy observation. He also knows that whoever gets to the ridge first shall be in a dominating position. He was aware that the enemy was probably trying to climb as well.

Around midnight, the moon slips behind dark clouds. Since the enemy cannot see them in the darkness, Sonam tells his men to move fast. Eleven of them start climbing, using their hands to pull themselves up as quickly as they can, rifles slung behind their backs. By the time the moon appears from behind the clouds, Sonam and his Ladakhi warriors are standing on top of the ridge, gasping for breath.

The Pakistanis are still directing prophylactic fire at their base camp every fifteen minutes. This is good news for the Ladakh Scouts. It means the Pakistanis do not know that they have climbed up. Sonam's party moves quietly along the ridge and discovers an enemy camp at a 40-metre drop from their position. They can see a tent with three sentries outside wearing camouflage white; even their rifles are covered in white making them very difficult to be spotted.

By then, Sonam's party with the MMG detachment, which had been trailing behind, shows up on the other side. The Pakistanis get sandwiched between the two teams of Ladakh Scouts.

The machine gunners open fire on the enemy camp below. The firefight continues through the night and till noon on 31 May. The enemy soldiers eventually lose their nerve.

Standing on the ridge, Sonam spots nearly sixty Pakistani soldiers below, folding their tents and withdrawing.

'We could see at least two platoons there but they managed to escape. We fired at them but they were out of our range. Since I had no radio communication with my base, we could not get artillery fire upon them either,' he recounts.

Soon the Ladakh Scouts run out of ammunition. They start rolling boulders down the slope. The enemy sentries who had taken cover inside their tents are crushed. The bodies of five other Pakistani soldiers killed in the crossfire lie on the ridge but the slope is so steep that Sonam's men cannot recover them to serve as proof to the media that Pakistan had a presence inside the LoC.

The Ladakh Scouts capture four Pakistani posts on the ridge. By then, besides ammunition, they have also run out of food. Since their radio set has also broken down, Sonam decides to go down to Handangbrok to get reinforcements.

Sonam and Rifleman Qadir start from the ridge at 5 p.m. Taking a tricky alternative route down through rocks and ice since they don't know if there are still some enemy posts from where they are being watched, they plod through snow and painstakingly climb down to their camp at Handangbrok.

———

Mission accomplished
31 May
11 p.m.
Handangbrok

Night has fallen when the two soldiers, dirty, bedraggled, tired and hungry, walk out of the valley bathed in the pale translucent rays of the waning moon and take the roadhead to their camp. Maj. Katoch is relieved to find them returning safe.

When Sonam informs him that the ridgeline has been cleared of the enemy, a smile of disbelief spreads across his stressed face. He hugs Sonam and Qadir and congratulates them on a job well done. Sonam tells him that they have come back to replenish ammunition and rations but before that they would like to eat because they are famished.

Steaming hot chow mein is immediately ordered from the cookhouse and the hungry warriors shove it into their mouths with loaded chopsticks. They drink big mugs of hot sugary tea and, energy levels up, decide to trek back to Area Rock Fall before sleep can claim them. Sonam fears that if they delay, the enemy might regroup and attempt a counter-attack.

Three sturdy mules are loaded with ammunition, rations and medicines; seven additional soldiers, fresh and spirited, are provided. At midnight the team starts back for the glacier. Their path is lit by the moon that has bathed the entire snow-capped landscape in a ghostly white glow. The soldiers are in no mood to enjoy the ethereal beauty of the terrain. They trudge on, one weary step after another, the route relatively familiar by now. They cross into the mouth of the mountainous semicircle where they were earlier ambushed by the enemy. It is silent now, but they remember Rigzin's bleeding body lying on a groundsheet on the snow. Their hearts grieve for the loss of their brave comrade.

By 5 a.m., they have reached the rest of their team, who are relieved to see food and ammunition.

'We spent the next fourteen days patrolling the area. On the enemy's side also we could see Pakistan Army patrols but they did not attempt another incursion,' Col. Wangchuk recounts.

The bodies of the three enemy soldiers who had been crushed in their tents are taken down, along with their I-cards and letters from home that prove beyond doubt that they were regular soldiers of the Pakistan Army. The battalion 14 Sikh is flown down from Delhi and its soldiers positioned in the secured areas. They take some time to realize that guns jam in the freezing temperatures and have to be thawed over stoves to get them working, but they go on to do very good work.

Finally, on 14 June, Sonam returns to Handangbrok. His task is complete and, having been granted seven days of casual leave, he is now on his way to Leh. In the officers mess at Dah, he is shown a copy of *India Today* that has a detailed article on Operation Rock Fall. It mentions that he has been recommended for a MVC, while three of his men have been recommended for VrCs.

Sonam reads it over a glass of rum with hot water and leaves for Leh the next morning. His wife, who he has not been in touch with for more than fifteen days, bursts into tears of relief when she sees him walking into the house. His ageing parents and sisters, who had been praying for him all these days, rush down to hug him in relief. His son, Riggyal, whose first birthday he missed on 11 June, looks at him with wide innocent eyes and gurgles happily. Sonam picks him up and holds his close to his heart, relieved that he has returned alive to the people he loves the most in the world.

An Army Band Comes Marching

'I spent most of that week in bed recovering from the intense physical and mental fatigue I had undergone. I would meet people who came to see me and then go back to my room to rest. Having my family around me was a blessing,' Col. Wangchuk says.

After his leave was over, he moved back to Karu and further up to his company position at Fukche. 'We watched the Kargil War unfold on our television sets and the victories that started coming to us one by one with great satisfaction,' he says. After the war is declared over on 26 July, Sonam goes back home on a longer leave.

One morning he is surprised by the celebratory sound of the Army band. He and his wife look out of the window and are surprised to find the band rhythmically making its way to their house through the thicket. Right in front is his CO, grinning widely.

'My MVC had been announced and they had come to congratulate me,' Col. Wangchuk recounts. India's second highest gallantry award was pinned to his shirtfront by the President in an investiture ceremony held at Rashtrapati Bhavan in February 2000. Before that, Sonam led the Ladakh Scouts, who proudly marched past their countrymen and smartly saluted the President in the Republic Day Parade on 26 January 2000. They had proved their dedication to duty by getting the country its first victory in the Kargil War.

Author's Note

For displaying exceptional bravery and gallantry of the highest order in the presence of enemy fire, (then) Maj. Sonam Wangchuk was awarded the Maha Vir Chakra. Hav. Tsewang Rigzin was buried in Hanuthang village, where a memorial now stands in his memory.

Story 1

Ladakhi Boys Turn Porters in War

6 June 1999
Leh

Ladakhis tune in to AIR Leh to listen to news about the ongoing war are surprised to hear an unusual announcement. '*Bharatiya sena ko apna samaan ladai mein le jaane ke liye volunteers chahiye. Aage aaiye, madad kariye. Desh ko aapki zarurat hai* [The Indian Army needs porters to carry loads to the front. Please come forward to help; the country needs you].' It is the clear voice of Mrs T. Angmo Shuno, station director, All India Radio (AIR), Leh and Kargil.

Through the following week, Mrs Angmo, a well-known figure in Leh, repeatedly requests families to send their able-bodied sons to the Leh Polo Ground, where selections

are being made. The announcements have been made on
the request of Col. Vinay Dutta, who visited Mrs Angmo
a day before and explained to her that he was recruiting
boys to raise a Pioneer company for meeting the needs of
assaulting battalions during war time.

'Col. Dutta told me that there were no roads in the
mountains and that the Indian Army did not have enough
porters or mules to carry food, ammunition and other
necessities to the battlefront. He asked me if I could help
by asking Ladakhi boys to volunteer for the task,' Mrs
Angmo remembers, speaking to me nineteen years later. 'I
assured him I would do everything I could to help.'

'The Indian Army is fighting for us; it is our turn to
help them,' she tells her listeners that morning, halting
scheduled broadcasts to repeat her message. To set an
example, she asks her youngest son, Stanzin Jaydun
(Ricky), who is eighteen and still in school, to volunteer for
the task. '*Main agar dusre logon ko bolun ki apne bacchon
ko war mein bhej do toh wo bolte tum apne bacche ko kyun
nahi bhejti* [How could I ask others to send their children
to the battlefront if I was not sending my own],' she says.
She explains this to Ricky, who was initially a little scared
but soon was convinced about going.

'Within four days, nearly 200 of us had volunteered to
go with the Army. Two platoons of 100 each were formed
and Army trucks took us to Biama, a small village between
Dah and Hanu, which was about an eight-hour drive from
Leh,' Ricky says. 'We were in the age group of eighteen to

thirty-five—fit, able and, most importantly, accustomed to the weather and the terrain.'

In Biama, farmers growing tomatoes in their fields were requested to give space for tents to be erected and a camp was set up on the step farms just below the road. By the end of the week, the number of volunteers had grown to 600.

For two months, the Ladakhi boys stayed there, coming to the aide of any infantry battalion that needed them. Requests came from Army units that were moving up to fight in the Batalik-Yaldor-Chorbat La sector, and the boys were dispatched in teams as per the requirements. While normal porters can carry a 10-kg load, the young Ladakhi boys carry as much as 30 kg easily. They were given daily wages but Ricky says most did it to serve the Army in whatever way they could.

'Some of the boys also helped in evacuating dead and injured soldiers; we all knew what a big price our soldiers were paying in the war. We wanted to do out bit,' he says.

Biama, where the boys had set up camp, was in the enemy's shelling zone. 'There was a water tank nearby and we would run and hide inside it whenever enemy shelling started,' Ricky says.

Radio in War

During the war, AIR Kargil was under constant threat of closure since local staff had to work under almost regular shelling, but thanks to Mrs Angmo's initiative, no one left.

Mrs Angmo remembers how she would always have a car and driver ready outside the AIR station.

'The moment shelling started, we would jump in and speed away to a small village called Mingi 15 km away, towards Zanskar, which was out of the enemy's shelling range. We had rented a room there and often all of us (staff of AIR Kargil) would sleep on the floor and then go back after the shelling stopped to continue with our radio transmissions,' she recollects.

The radio station played a big role in controlling rumours and propaganda perpetrated by Radio Pakistan. 'They would broadcast outrageous lies that had to be countered. Radio Pakistan would claim that so many Indian soldiers had been killed that the stench from their bodies was forcing civilians to leave their villages,' Mrs Angmo remembers. 'When some of our choppers developed snags, Radio Pakistan started broadcasting that they had shot down Indian Army choppers. Once a shell fell on the Kargil Dak Bangla. Within half an hour Radio Pakistan claimed that the Dak Bangla had been destroyed. They even propagated these lies in Shina language, which is spoken in India by the people living in Dras and Gurez; and in Pakistan in Gilgit and Baltistan.'

Mrs Angmo says it became necessary to counter these lies and AIR Kargil did so very effectively by broadcasting regular programmes in both Hindi as well as Shina. Besides quelling rumours, the radio station played an important role in boosting the morale of the soldiers; it sent messages of encouragement to soldiers on the front, read out notes from their families telling them to fight bravely and not worry about home, and even asked local people to spare mules to carry the Army's loads to the heights where the battles were going on.

'Often as many as 300 shells would land in Kargil in a day but we continued to work. The radio station was not closed even for a single day through the war though often the Army would tell us to switch off all lights at night to ensure we didn't get bombed. We would close windows and draw the curtains before switching on any light,' Mrs Angmo remembers.

She recollects one particular evening when there was so much shelling that the engineers at AIR Kargil ran away. 'Our broadcast was to begin at 5 p.m., but there was no one to start the generators. I had to call up the Brigade Commander at Kargil for help. He immediately sent some soldiers who started the generator and we could finally begin our broadcast at 8 p.m.,' she says.

There were no awards for Mrs Angmo and her team after the war but she remembers with pride how the then information and broadcasting minister Pramod Mahajan, who kept touring border areas to visit Doordarshan and AIR offices during the war, saw them working tirelessly and complimented them by saying that while the soldiers were fighting on the border, the media was fighting at its own level. The minister also visited a command base hospital in Srinagar where injured soldiers were recovering.

There he noticed that they did not have access to any entertainment. According to an *India Today* report (dated 26 July 1999), thirty colour television sets, 1000 transistors and a computer were organized for the patients through private donors.

Author's Note

Mrs T. Angmo Shuno is now retired. She and Ricky continue to live in Leh.

Chapter 3

Haneef

In the freezing heights of Turtuk, much above where Shyok—the river of death—flows, is a battlefield named after a young Muslim officer.

August 1998
Karu, Ladakh

It is a cold winter evening when Col. Anil Bhatia, CO, 11 Rajputana Rifles (Raj. Rif.), sets out in his jonga to go to the Ladakh Scouts Training Centre Mess in Leh. He is accompanied, along with other officers of the unit, by twenty-five-year-old Capt. Haneef-ud-din, cheerful, handsome and politely attentive.

The battalion has been busy training for its tenure at the Siachen Glacier but this is a rare relaxed evening.

They have been invited for dinner. While drinks are being served, the Ladakh Scouts Jazz Band entertains its guests by playing one foot-tapping number after another. Col. Bhatia walks up to Capt. Haneef, who is standing quietly in a corner, and puts an affectionate arm around the young officer.

'*Ja yaar, tu bhi inko kuch suna de* [Go on, sing something for them],' he says.

'Right, sir,' Haneef smiles and, placing his soft drink on the bar counter, walks up to the band.

From across the room, a glass of whiskey in hand, Col. Bhatia watches, smiling indulgently as Haneef asks for a guitar, adjusts the mike and starts singing, '*Lakhon hain yahan dilwale, par pyaar nahin milta.*'

Haneef's rich, sonorous voice fills up the room, making the ladies smile and the officers sit up and take notice. Idle chatter comes to a stop and by the time the evening is over almost everyone is under the spell of this young officer with a beautiful voice. Col. Bhatia is still humming those songs when he is driven back by Haneef later that night.

'*Tune toh aaj bade fans bana liye mere singer-soldier* [You acquired many fans this evening, my singer-soldier],' he says looking fondly at his officer.

Haneef just smiles his shy smile, hands on the steering, careful eyes on the road curving ahead.

A few months later, Haneef is dead.

Turtuk
2018

Nineteen years have passed since the Kargil War. The Shyok, river of death in Yarkandi Uyghur, meanders through these vast forgotten lands before slipping into Pakistan and merging with the Indus at Skardu. Adjacent to Subsector Haneef, named after the young officer who was martyred here at the age of twenty-five, stands a small mosque. Above the green lands, where apricot orchards grow and chubby children with alabaster skin and apple-pink cheeks play, is an icy wilderness bordered by the formidable Karakoram Range.

This is where Capt. Haneef-ud-din, pulling his sinewy body forward, crawled, rifle in hand, in the snow on 6 June 1999. He died on this craggy mountainside exactly two years after he had passed out of the IMA. It is poignant that this young boy with a Hindu mother and a Muslim father, who grew up celebrating both Eid and Diwali, died in a war between two countries that had been split on the basis of communal ideologies. He had gone to fight for 11 Raj. Rif. whose war cry is 'Raja Ram Chandra ki Jai'.

Haneef's body lay under the open sky and falling snow for forty-three days, his handsome face frozen into a cold mask. When then Army Chief Gen. Ved Prakash Malik visited Mrs Hema Aziz, Haneef's mother, in her small Mayur Vihar apartment in Delhi and told her the body could not be retrieved because the enemy was firing constantly, she met his eyes bravely and said she did not want another soldier to risk his life to get her son's body back.

'After the war is over I would like to go and see where he died,' she said.

Gen. Malik assured her that she would be able to.

Haneef's body was eventually retrieved. He was buried with full military honours in Delhi. Mrs Hema Aziz made the pilgrimage with her other two sons to Turtuk, going all the way to see where her son, who used to laughingly complain that she never had time for him, had given up his life for his country. This time, he was not around to see her.

———

December 2018
Defence Services Officers Institute (DSOI)
Dhaula Kuan, Delhi

'Haneef, or Haneefu as many of us affectionately called him, was the youngest officer in my battalion. He was soft-spoken and energetic, and always the first to volunteer for any task. He was excellent at computers and a very good singer. In fact, he had set up a jazz band for our unit, carting equipment all the way from Delhi. The band, called Haneef Band, still exists,' Col. Anil Bhatia, who has now retired, tells me over sandwiches and coffee that

Mrs Monika Bhatia has ordered for us at the restaurant inside DSOI where we are sitting.

Leaning forward on his chair, his eyes clouded with memories of the war that still wake him up on cold winter nights, Col. Bhatia goes on to tell me a heartbreaking story of courage and sacrifice, of how Haneef was lost and the men of 11 Raj. Rif. conquered one of the greatest heights of Turtuk to avenge his death.

The story begins soon after Capt. Haneef and his company come down from Siachen Glacier after completing their four-month tenure at the glacier often referred to as the highest battlefield in the world; the LoC ends there and is still disputed between India and Pakistan.

Haneef is at the base camp functioning as load manifest officer, monitoring the maintenance and air supply of rations, medicines, letters etc. to various posts on the glacier. Ideally, soldiers who come down from the gruelling Siachen tenure are given a rest period in Panamic Hot Sulphur Springs, near Partapur village, or sent home on leave. However, the Kargil War has changed this. The Army unit deployed in Turtuk sector—12 Jat—has reported an enemy intrusion and since no fresh troops are readily available because of the war currently raging in Batalik sector, men are being sourced from the Army units that are around. This is the time when orders are passed that an officer-led platoon from 11 Raj. Rif. should be sent to Turtuk to help assess the extent of enemy intrusion. Maj. Ranjit Singh takes the first ad hoc company (of about sixty men). Later, the unit is asked to provide another ad hoc company, which moves to Turtuk under Maj. Sanjay Vishwas Rao.

Early May 1999
Turtuk

The soldiers of 11 Raj. Rif. are loaded in trucks that speed along the fast-flowing Shyok. Most of them have just come down from Siachen while some have reported back from leave. The tarred road is flanked by magnificent grey mountains on both sides. It would have been a fascinating journey had the soldiers not been heading for action. The men are grim but not complaining.

An unperturbed Haneef sits beside the driver, happily humming a song. He does not know yet what task he is heading for but he knows that additional troops will be used to send out fifteen patrols to Subsector West to identify and clear enemy intrusion across the LoC.

Since the enemy has established posts on the LoC, 11 Raj. Rif. is asked to acquire positions on the intermediate ridge and gather information since their strength is not enough to launch an attack yet. The troops reach Turtuk and then move self-contained for seven days along Turtuk Nullah.

As the soldiers climb higher, the landscape becomes increasingly inhospitable. Signs of civilization, or even tracks to follow, are few and far between. The entire area from Turtuk to Chorbat La is dotted with deadly crevasses where one wrong step can send a man plunging to his death. Winds cut like whetted knives and avalanches can kill in seconds. The soldiers are not in communication with anyone after they cross Zangpal, a small post with a makeshift helipad, about 6 km before the mouth of the Karchen Glacier. They are adapted to living in the glacier and they use that experience to negotiate the tough terrain.

Wading through thigh-high snow in subzero temperatures, they finally reach the intermediate ridge where they acquire features and set up temporary positions. All three officers are stationed there with their troops. The men start building up stocks for the impending attack, ferrying ammunition and rations on their backs, and also carry out patrols in the area.

On 6 June, Haneef volunteers to take a daytime patrol to the Karchen Glacier. He decides to get closer to the enemy, provoking them to fire so that he can mark their location. This will help identify the position of enemy bunkers and automatic weapons, which will be useful when an attack is finally launched.

Accompanied by Naib Subedar Mangej Singh and around seven Other Ranks, Haneef crosses a location called Ledge, skirts the Karchen Glacier and gets within 300 metres of the enemy. The patrol identifies eight enemy *sanghar*s (roughly made bunkers) and deployment of automatic weapons on Point 5590 and Area Saddle (the two posts occupied by Pakistan on the LoC). This critical information, without which future attacks would not have been possible, comes from the surviving members of Haneef's team. Haneef does not, unfortunately, realize that he has gone too far and is now under direct enemy observation.

Targetting Haneef and his men, the enemy rains devastating fire on them. A screaming Naib Subedar Mangej is lifted in the air and thrown into a bottomless crevasse. Haneef and Rifleman Parvesh are also hit. Falling to his knees, his body rocked by unbearable pain, Haneef watches in disbelief as Parvesh drops his rifle and falls on the snow, blood spilling on to the landscape. His own hand unclasps to let go of his rifle and he falls in a pool of blood in the snow. Above him, white cumulous clouds waft across the brilliant blue sky. He feels a suffocating tightness in his chest. He can sense that life is ebbing away. His vital organs are shutting down. He closes his eyes and waits for the pain to end. Cold winds lash his body, but Haneef cannot feel anything any more. His breathing slows down and finally stops. Haneef dies, twenty-five years old, hundreds of miles from home and loved ones.

The rest of the men take cover behind boulders and try to return the fire but their small arms are no match for the enemy's arsenal. Frantic efforts are made to retrieve the bodies but the constant barrage of enemy shelling does not allow them to. Finally, they give up and return to Zangpal. All later efforts to extricate the bodies also fail.

———

'We Shall Retrieve the Bodies of Our Martyrs'

By 7 July, nearly a month after Haneef dies, 11 Raj. Rif. completes its Siachen tenure and is de-inducted from the glacier. Col. Bhatia is furious about the loss of his men and is raging like an injured lion. The unit reaches Turtuk on 10 July. Col. Bhatia moves to Zangpal, takes a week to study the position of the enemy posts, and then gives himself his first task.

'We shall retrieve the bodies of our martyrs,' he tells his men. Operation Amar Shaheed is launched. On 18 July, forty-three days after Haneef dies, Capt. S.K. Dhiman, Maj. Sanjay Vishwas Rao, Lt Ashish Bhalla, Hav. Surinder and Rifleman Dharam Vir volunteer for the task and leave Zangpal at last light, crossing over to the glacier nearly 6 km away.

Carefully negotiating the deadly precipices, the soldiers manage to locate Haneef and Parvesh, and extricate the frozen bodies. Dragging them behind boulders, and then carrying them on their backs, they walk quietly through the night, reaching Zangpal by 7 a.m. A helicopter lands the next morning and carries the bodies away as Col. Bhatia watches the body bags with moist eyes. Subedar Mangesh's body still lies in a crevasse.

'We will get you soon, Mangesh,' Col. Bhatia makes a silent promise to the dead soldier. That promise is fulfilled when the battle is finally over.

The troops of 11 Raj. Rif. now plan to avenge the deaths of their comrades by attacking and capturing Point 5590. Col. Bhatia starts planning the assault on Point 5590 which is to be called Operation Haneef. By 24 July, the unit is ready to attack but since it is a full-moon period, a decision is taken to delay the attack by a few more days so that troops have the advantage of darkness. General Officer Commanding (GOC), 3 Div., Maj. Gen. Padam Budhwar lands at Zangpal in a helicopter and okays the war plan. Col. Bhatia makes a request for Bofors fire and mortars at Turtuk to soften the enemy, which is approved by the GOC. Meanwhile, the soldiers stock up rations and ammunition and carry out route reconnaissance for the impending attack.

———

Operation Haneef
2 August 1999
6.45 p.m.
Base of Karchen Glacier

The mountains are dark and silent, but on the glacier, where the ice has frozen to a slippery sheet, reflected light makes any movement visible to the enemy sitting on the heights. That is why Col. Bhatia has decided that his men will not climb over the glacier but take the more difficult route along its base to climb up to Point 5590 from the rear. They will climb from the side facing Pakistan. It will be tougher, he knows, but it will also give his men the advantage of surprise since Pakistan would never expect an attack from that side.

He has waited nine days after full moon to ensure that the night is dark enough. For the past three days, the enemy posts have been bombarded from the firebases established for the attack. The Bofors guns at Kargil target the heights and the Faggot missile launchers at the firebases attempt to directly hit enemy bunkers. The most effective fire, however, comes from 11 Raj. Rif.'s own 81 mm mortar and the 120 mm mortar tube that the soldiers have carried on their backs to a position established short of Karchen Glacier. Not only is the gun heavy, every bomb weighs 15 kg.

The Attack

Nearly forty men, all volunteers, have been split up into two groups. Task Force 1 is made of Bravo Company, which shall be the leading company under Capt. Anirudh Chauhan, a trained mountaineer. The group also includes five soldiers from Vikas (a Special Frontier Forces battalion) who are experts at rock climbing and rope-fixing. Task Force 2 comprises men from Charlie Company, led by Lt Ashish Bhalla. Task Forces 3 and 4 are to follow.

Coming from Siachen, the soldiers have glacier clothing and shoes but the fatigue of living in subzero temperatures for three months at a stretch is evident. Almost all of them have lost considerable weight and muscle. Lingering headaches and forgetfulness are common, as are blood pressure fluctuations. But they make no excuses.

'*Upar Point 5590 dikhai de raha hai aapko* [Can you see Point 5590]'? Col. Bhatia asks, standing in the freezing cold that turns his face red and makes his warm breath come out in bursts of steam.

'*Dushman ne wahin se fire kar ke hamare saathiyon ko mara tha. Jaiye unhe dikhaiye, 11 Raj. Rif. apne bhaiyon ki maut ka badla kaise leti hai,*' [That's where the enemy shot and killed our comrades from. Go and show them how we avenge the deaths of our brothers],' Col. Bhatia thunders.

With the battle cry of 'Raja Ram Chandra ki Jai,' the men start walking. They circle the glacier and reach the foot of the towering moonlit mountains that appear dark, eerie and suffused in strange shadows. At nearly 18,340 feet, Post 5590 is the highest point.

Breathless from exertion, fingers frozen in the cold, the men struggle to find footholds. Rocks crumble under their feet, sending debris down the slope. Being crushed under a dislodged boulder is as much of a risk as taking a wrong step and plummeting down to a gory death. The soldiers encounter a steep rock face but the boys of Vikas Regiment use their expertise to fix ropes which the soldiers climb to reach 40 metres short of the top.

They have been climbing for about nine hours and are bone-tired. It is 4 a.m. and another 80-degree incline stands before them. They convey this to Col. Bhatia, who is stationed at the base of the Karchen Glacier.

'I asked them to turn back. As soon as the sun came up, they as well as the teams following them would be spotted by the enemy located on the surrounding posts. The risk was not worth taking,' recounts Col. Bhatia. 'Disheartened, the teams turn back. It takes them two hours to get down and they are exhausted by then. They were so tired that they just dropped down wherever they could find place, closed their eyes and went to sleep. We could not offer them anything in the name of food or warmth. All we had were stale shakkarparas (a fried snack made from flour and sugar that doesn't go bad for a long time), two small snow tents and the shelter of boulders,' he says sadly.

The soldiers try to rest till evening. And then it is time to make a second attempt.

———

The final attack
3 August 1999
6 p.m.

Col. Bhatia calls for the soldiers to line-up in the freezing cold. The men are tired and hungry but the attack has to take place. He asks for volunteers once again.

'I was a little apprehensive this time. The reason was not because my men were not brave; they were. It was because they were so fatigued that I knew they just did not have the required physical strength,' Col. Bhatia tells me, matter of fact, that winter afternoon in the DSOI.

Standing in the biting wind, Col. Bhatia reminds the soldiers that Haneef's death needs to be avenged. '*Hum agar ye kaam pura kiye bina wapis jaayenge toh log kya kahenge?*' [What will people say if we go back without doing this task?] he says gravely. '*Woh bolenge Gyarah Raj. Rif. apne saathiyon ki maut ka badla liye bina wapis aa gayi. Yeh humari paltan ki izzat ka sawaal hai. Hume apne saathiyon ki maut ka badla lena hai. Mujhe volunteer chahiye. Kaun jayega?* [They will say that 11 Raj. Rif. has returned without avenging the death of its comrades. This is a matter of our honour. We have to exact retribution for their death. I want volunteers. Who will go?],' Col. Bhatia says looking his men in the eye, his voice as cold as the wind.

There is a long silence while the wind screams and the peaks stand silent. Then a gruff voice comes through in the falling dusk, '*Sahab, main jaoonga* [I will go, Sir],' Naib Subedar Abhay Singh, a basketball player from Bravo Company, steps forward.

Soon, other men start looking up to meet Col. Bhatia's gaze. Amongst the initial volunteers are boxer Dilbagh Singh, cross-country runners Ajit, Rajesh and Chand Bir, bodybuilder Kishen Kumar, Rifleman Durga Ram and Havildar Kaan Singh. All of them had been part of the earlier aborted attack also.

Gradually, more men start stepping up. The really fatigued troops are replaced by fresh ones and the brave ones start their arduous climb once again. The same two officers—Anirudh Chauhan and Ashish Bhalla—lead the teams.

Anirudh and Task Force 1, climbing in a single file, manage to reach the base of Point 5590 just before midnight. But they are again face-to-face with the 80-degree gradient. This time they fix ropes and by 5.30 a.m. manage to climb on to a jutting overhang.

The sky is getting lighter. Above them, they can see three enemy sanghars, one of which has the barrel of a machine gun jutting out of the loophole. Sitting on that ledge, they call their CO on the radio set. The enemy is barely 25 metres away. Col. Bhatia advises the team to stay hidden behind rocks through the day and attack after last light to avoid a counter-attack from surrounding enemy posts.

Around 5.45 p.m., Col. Bhatia gets a desperate message from Anirudh. '*Sir, shayad unko shak ho gaya hai* [Sir, perhaps they suspect our presence]. They are firing in our direction,' he says.

'The sun will go down soon. There is no other way but to charge physically,' Col. Bhatia tells Anirudh. 'Be brave, my boys,' he adds, his heart heavy with concern.

A Fierce Hand-to-Hand Battle

Many men stand out for their selfless bravery and sacrifice that night. Hav. Kishen Kumar takes the initiative when the enemy starts firing at his team. When others hesitate to go up and fix the machine gun, he volunteers, stepping boldly into enemy fire and emerging, miraculously, unhurt.

Anirudh and Naib Subedar Abhay Singh lead. Kaan Singh volunteers to go first in the daring attack, knowing fully well that he is putting his life at risk. Shouting 'Raja Ram Chandra ki Jai,' he charges bravely at the enemy soldiers, flinging a grenade.

A bullet catches him in the neck and he falls off the edge of the post. Dilbagh leaps to get a hold on his comrade but can only catch his rifle. Kaan Singh drops into the gaping mouth of a crevasse. His eyes brimming over with tears of helplessness, Dilbagh rushes forward and lunges at the enemy soldiers. A fierce hand-to-hand battle rages at Point 5590 through the night.

Naib Subedar Abhay Singh displays exemplary valour as well. To mislead the enemy into believing that he has many more than ten men with him, he keeps shouting out instructions like '*Aadhe mere piche aao, thode aadmi daayen se jao, baaki baayen se jao. Aage badho* [Half of you come with me; some attack from the right, the other half from the left].' Not only does he inspire his own men to fight bravely, he also fools the enemy into thinking that they have been attacked by a full company of as many as 100 men.

Meanwhile, to support his troops, Col. Bhatia orders all available weapons from the firebases, including missiles and rocket launchers, to fire upon the enemy's surrounding posts, with the exception of Point 5590. The fire continues till 8 p.m. providing cover to the climbing troops of Task Forces 3 and 4, who are to join the attacking company.

Meanwhile Task Force 1 is at its job. After silencing the machine gun, two more sanghars are captured and three enemy soldiers killed. Task Force 2 catches up with them and fixes ropes over the blade's edge of Point 5590 to drop down on to Area Saddle where they can spot sanghars and ten more enemy soldiers. Rifle shots, war cries and screams of the injured pierce the silence of the dark night. Col. Bhatia and the rest can hear the guns and see flashes on the mountain but they have no idea of how their comrades are faring.

Col. Bhatia has switched off his own radio connection with 102 Brigade Headquarter, Partapur, since he wants to avoid unnecessary interference. 'It was highly distracting since they were so far away and we could not have waited for or followed their instructions. We had to handle the battle on our own.' He switches it on only around 5 a.m. after he is told that both Point 5590 and Area Saddle have been captured.

Seven enemy soldiers have been killed, the rest have fled to Pakistan. The victorious soldiers return with seventeen captured enemy weapons, including heavy machine guns, rocket launchers, RC guns, and anti-aircraft missiles that they carry on their backs 18 kilometres to Turtuk. The weapons are then taken to Partapur in vehicles to be displayed during a visit by then defence minister George Fernandez.

Though a very high casualty rate had been expected, 11 Raj. Rif. loses one man in this operation. This in spite of the fact that the unit had been at a complete disadvantage—the soldiers were fatigued and were climbing up to fight a well-established enemy, they had no intelligence on how many soldiers waited for them on the heights and with what weapons.

Since the war has been declared over by the time this daring operation takes place, the unit does not get many gallantry awards.

'We avenged our comrades, that was our greatest reward,' says Col. Bhatia, sipping his coffee as we close the interview. He has retired but his elder son, Nishchay, who was ten when his father fought the war, has joined 11 Raj. Rif. and is a Major now. When I interview Col. Bhatia, he has just returned from the passing out parade of his younger son who was only three during the war. Lt Manak has been commissioned into 9 Raj. Rif.

One Haneef might have gone, but the brave young soldier shall keep inspiring many more.

———

December 2018
Kargil Apartments
Dwarka

It is a cold foggy morning when I park my car and call Mrs Hema Aziz for directions to her flat.

'I am on the upper floor,' she says.

I look up to find a graceful, elderly lady in a black salwar kameez smiling down at me from the first floor. She invites me into her modestly furnished flat where a photograph of Capt. Haneef-ud-din, VrC, in uniform looks at us from an otherwise bare wall. A portrait sits on a bookshelf, his handsome face flanked by the Tricolour, a gift from artist Hutansh Verma who paints portraits of martyrs and hand delivers them to their families.

The door to the balcony is open, allowing Delhi's winter chill inside. My fingers feel like wood as I take down notes but Mrs Aziz doesn't seem to notice the cold. More than once, during that conversation that stretched into a few hours, I wanted to request her to close the door but each time I was reminded that her son's body lay in the snow for forty-three days, and keep quiet instead.

'Soldiers Don't Go to the Battlefield to Die'

Haneef was born on 23 August 1974 and was brought up in Old Delhi by his grandmother. Both his parents worked with the song and drama division of the ministry of information and broadcasting—his father was a theatre artiste and his mother a classical singer. They would often tour the country, performing for soldiers posted in the border areas.

'It was satisfying work but we could not be with the children in their early years,' explains Mrs Aziz. Haneef was brought up almost entirely by his grandmother till he was eight. He would get up at 6 a.m. with her every day, after which she would take him along for whatever morning chores she had to do. 'He remained an early riser. He never needed an alarm to get up in the morning even when he started going to college,' she says.

Haneef was twenty-two when he came to his mother with the indemnity bond she would have to sign before he joined the IMA. 'When I started reading it, he said, "*Padh kyun rahi ho, bas sign kar do na* [Why are you reading it. Just sign it]",' Mrs Hema Aziz recollects. 'When I told him that I wanted to know what document I was signing, he said, "It's a bond that says you will get nothing if something happens to me during the training." I told him, "It is your dream to join the Army. I will never stop you."'

She says Haneef had been offered a job with the computer firm he was training with when his call came for the Army. 'He sat down with me and asked me what I thought he should do now that he had two job offers in hand.' She says she reminded him of how happy he had been when he had gone for the Allahabad Service Selection Board (SSB). Four of his friends had also gone for the SSB but only he had got selected. 'Anyone can work with a computer firm but only you are getting a chance to serve your nation,' she had told him. Haneef decided to join the Army.

He was used to taking his own decisions. His father, Aziz-ud-din Effendi, had succumbed to a massive heart attack when Haneef was just eight and his elder brother, Nafees, ten. Mrs Aziz had brought up the boys as a single mother, sending her youngest son, Sameer, to live with her sister in Bangalore. Since she had started working with Kathak Kendra, Delhi, she would often be singing for renowned artistes like Pandit Birju Maharaj, Yamini Krishnamurthy and Swapna Sundari, and often had to travel with them for their performances. Haneef was ten and Nafees twelve when she had to go on a Europe tour, leaving them alone in the small house they had shifted into after their father's death. 'They knew they did not have a father and their mother had to work to support them so they never complained. I gave them pocket money and left extra money with the neighbours in case there was an emergency. It was a one-and-a-half-month tour that stretched to three months. They managed on their own,' she says smiling nostalgically. 'They both paid their school fees, went to school on time, managed their food and ironed their clothes. Haneef could even make paranthas at that age.'

She shares an incident when Haneef had come back from school and happily told her that he was going to get a free uniform since he did not have a father. She had told him to refuse it saying, 'Tell your teacher that my mother earns enough and can afford to buy my uniform.' She had explained to him that in most families only fathers brought home salaries and that was why those children needed economic support if their father died. 'You are not entitled to that free uniform because your mother earns,' she told her wide-eyed son who nodded and told his teacher what his mother had said. Nearly a decade later, she refused the gas agency that was offered to her by the central government as a Kargil martyr's mother, saying she was a musician and would not be able to run it. Since it was in Haneef's name, she did not think it would be right on her part to pass it on to someone else to run.

'It Was His Destiny'

'Soldiers don't go to the battlefield to die, they go to fight. Haneef had opted to be a soldier. He had taken a pledge to always place his country before his own self; he had to honour it,' Mrs Aziz tells me, her face soft yet firm. 'I am proud of my son. There cannot be a greater statement on his valour than his death which came while fighting the enemy. There are so many soldiers who came back alive from the war. I am happy for them. It was Haneef's destiny to not return and I accept it. He has been an inspiration to so many. Even though his life was short, it was meaningful,' she says.

Mrs Hema Aziz lives alone in her apartment in Delhi. She does not take music classes any more but every morning, strains of the tanpura waft out of her open window as she sits doing her *riyaaz*. This is the time when she closes her eyes and is lost in a world that is still beautiful for her; where her son Haneef probably smiles again.

Author's Note

The initial intrusion in Turtuk sector was detected by a patrol of 12 Jat. The main battle was fought later by 11 Raj. Rif. during July–August 1999, ending when the unit captured Point 5590. Due to lack of communication and rugged terrain, these operations were not covered by the media in detail and thus never came into the public eye. Taken from Kargil 1999 – The Impregnable Conquered *written by Lt Gen. Y.M. Bammi.*

For his gallant action and bravery of an exceptionally high order in the face of the enemy, Capt. Haneef-ud-din was awarded the Vir Chakra posthumously and Subsector West was renamed Subsector Haneef in his honour. Capt. Anirudh Chauhan and Rifleman Kishen Kumar were awarded Sena Medals for their inspiring bravery.

Chapter 4

The Last Letter

A twenty-two-year-old going on a dangerous mission, from where return is uncertain, leaves behind a letter for his parents.

29 June 1999
2 a.m.
Knoll, Dras

Lieutenant Vijyant Thapar lies sprawled behind a rough cover of large boulders. Spreadeagled, he peers through the sight of his rifle. Beside him, Naik Tilak Singh has raised himself on his elbows and is pushing a magazine into his LMG. The moon is behind them, a huge milky disc of haunting beauty that is in sheer contrast to the bloodbath below. Its light reflects off the bare rocks, bathing the soldiers in a soft grey glow.

The battle has been raging through the night. The first two enemy positions have been captured. The third lies before them, so close yet frustratingly out of reach. A constant stream of enemy machine gun fire is ricocheting off the rock shielding them, preventing them from moving forward on the narrow ridgeline that can take just two soldiers at a time. Vijyant has had enough of the debilitating stalemate. Seething with tightly controlled fury, he decides to silence the gun that is keeping his men from advancing.

His sense of survival dictates that he stay behind cover but Vijyant has always been a man ruled by the heart. Unmindful of the danger he is putting himself in, he waits for a lull in the fire and then steps out. He takes careful aim at the enemy machine gunner and lets fly a stream of bullets.

Bathed in moonlight, he is spotted by a Pakistani sniper sitting on a cliff. The sniper cocks his rifle, takes careful aim and shoots. A bullet whips through the air and pierces Vijyant's left temple. The metal burns its way through his brain and comes out through his right eye.

A stunned Tilak Singh watches the young officer fall. Letting go of his own LMG, he crawls out and pulls Thapar back. Warm blood spills on the grey rocks. Vijyant's jacket is soaked from the bleeding wound but there is not a single scratch on his handsome face. His head falls to one side, his helmet rolls over exposing his black *patka* (a piece of cloth covering the head) and his eyes shut as he breathes his last in his comrade's arms.

The valiant Lt Vijyant Thapar, or Robin as his parents called him, is dead at just twenty-two. Six months ago, he had passed out of the IMA, proudly shaking hands with his father and hugging his tearful mother. That moment had marked the fulfilment of his childhood dream of wearing the uniform. In the battle of Knoll, he proved just how worthy he was of that honour.

———

29 June 2018
12 noon
Knoll

The rocky grey hills where the late Lt Vijyant Thapar, VrC, fought a bloody battle nineteen years ago are calm. The sky is an aquamarine blue, the air is crystal clear and you can feel it going right into your lungs.

It is hard to believe that one full moon night, grenades, gunfire and young human blood fell upon these very rocks. If you happen to visit, you will find old rusted rifle shells scattered here at 16,000 feet, mute witnesses to the fierce battle once fought. This is the spot where Thapar breathed his last. And this is where his father, seventy-three-year-old retired Col. (retd) Virender Thapar, now sits barefoot, his legs crossed and hands folded, participating in a havan held in memory of his son. His mind throws a flashback at him. A little boy with a grime-stained face and hair falling on his sweaty forehead is racing across a lush green lawn, a stick held in his hands like a rifle. His dog is following him at breakneck speed. The two are trying to scare monkeys off the stone boundary wall of an old British-era bungalow.

'Robin,' Col. Thapar whispers softly. His eyes are moist. The Army panditji sitting across him is chanting mantras in Sanskrit. Long orange flames leap out of the havan *kund*, bathing Col. Thapar's finely lined face in a warm red glow. Just five metres away is the stone sanghar where the young lieutenant fought his last battle. It has been converted into a temple where goddess Karni Mata generously shares space with Vijyant's photographs and a red dupatta that his mother sends from Delhi to be replaced every year.

For Col. Thapar, who comes here each year to commemorate the death anniversary of his son, this is the place where his heart finds peace. Some of that peace comes from the fact that he is respecting a wish Robin had made in the last letter he wrote home from the battlefield, knowing that he might never come back. 'If you can, please come and see where the Indian Army fought for your tomorrow,' he had written. And though it is becoming more and more difficult for Col. Thapar to make the treacherous climb to Knoll every passing year, he plans to honour that commitment for as long as he can.

His Last Letter

'Dearest Papa, Mama, Birdie and Granny,' begins the last letter that Vijyant wrote to his family from Kargil in June 1999. 'By the time you get this letter I'll be observing you from the sky, enjoying the hospitality of apsaras. I have no regrets. In fact, if I am reborn as a human I will join the army again and fight for my nation,' he writes on the purple Forces Inland letter, his neat right-slanted handwriting filling up the page. 'If you can, please come and see where the Indian Army fought for your tomorrow.' He adds that whatever organ can, should be taken; he asks his parents to donate money to an orphanage and asks them to give Rs 50 every month to Ruksana, a three-year-old Kashmiri girl he had befriended in Kashmir during his short stint there. He hopes that the sacrifice made by him and his men will not be forgotten by his battalion and his country. He signs off with a brave, 'OK, then it's time for me to join my clan of the Dirty Dozen. My assault party has twelve chaps. Live life kingsize. Your, Robin.'

Vijyant had written this letter to his family just a few days before he went to battle. It had been given to his parents with all his belongings packed in a black tin trunk, after his death. In fact, all the soldiers who had volunteered to go for this battle knew that the mission was risky and that they might not return. Some of them had left behind letters for loved ones, to be handed over if they did not come back. Vijyant was one of them. He had been told he was going to lead the attack. He must have guessed that his chances of survival were slim.

Here is the story of the late Lt Vijyant Thapar, VrC; pieced together from interviews with Col. Praveen Tomar, his coursemate who was with him in the war; Subedar Maj. Bhupinder Singh, who fought beside him in Knoll; and his parents, Col. and Mrs Thapar, who so generously shared not just his last letter, his diaries, his pictures, war reports and other documents, but also their precious memories with me.

May 2018,
Vijyant Enclave,
Noida

It is a warm summer morning when I get off the metro at the Botanical Garden station. Vijyant Enclave is easy to locate and I walk across to its front gate where a signboard pays homage to the brave young soldier whose parents I have come to interview.

When I ring the bell at the Thapar residence, a distinguished-looking, formally dressed Col. Virender Thapar holds the door open for me with a smile.

'Do authors look like this?' he asks, a twinkle in his eye. He is the quintessential Army officer, well dressed, well mannered, pleasant, charming and chivalrous. 'I was expecting someone older,' he says leading me inside to their beautifully done-up sitting room where Mrs Tripta Thapar gracefully steps forward and gives me a warm hug.

In so many ways life has moved on for the Thapars. They joke, they smile, they entertain guests and they talk about their older son with deep affection. So much so that if you didn't know it already, you would think that he had just stepped out for a chore and would be back soon. Yet, you soon realize that in so many ways life came to a stop for them the day Vijyant fell.

'The battle was a resounding success but we lost our son,' Col. Thapar says. 'We could have spent a life of gloom but that would have demeaned his martyrdom. So we broke through it and decided to use Robin's sacrifice to inspire the youth of India. We have been doing that ever since and it is satisfying to know that he has become a role model for future generations of officers.'

Later, Col. Thapar shows me around the house, taking me to Vijyant's room, which the Thapars have left untouched. He shows me his bed, his favourite books that line the study table, his posters that are still on the wall; his uniform hangs in a corner, his watch, beret and diary are neatly arranged in a glass cupboard. Through the afternoon, Mrs Thapar opens albums and shares with me pictures of the son who will remain twenty-two for them; they read out to me letters he wrote to them, they share with me their memories of the boy who always dreamt of joining the armed forces.

Gradually, the late Lt Vijyant Thapar, VrC, is no
longer just a name or story for me. He becomes Robin,
the young boy who would doodle soldiers and airplanes
in his rough notebook when he was supposed to be doing
math; who had once come home from the institute
soaking wet after a rain dance and had pacified his
annoyed father by telling him that he had danced with
none less than the then Miss India Manpreet Brar, who
had insisted that his mother continue to make for him
the cakes and chocolates he loved so much even after he
had joined the IMA.

'He was really close to his mother and he just loved
chocolates,' Col. Thapar says, narrating an incident linked
to a picture that has even gone into 2 Raj. Rif.'s regimental
history. The picture has a smiling Vijyant and Maj.
Padmapani Acharya sitting on Barbaad Bunker after their
first victory in Tololing. He tells me that when the CO,
Lt Col. M.B. Ravindranath, climbed up to meet his
victorious soldiers, a grinning Robin offered him a
chocolate he had fished out from his pocket. 'His pockets
were always filled with chocolates,' he says smiling fondly.

Mrs Thapar tells me how she and Col. Thapar had
rushed to the Tughlakabad railway station with a big cake
to meet the military special train that was taking Robin and
his battalion from Gwalior to Kashmir a few months before
the war started, but had got late. She remembers how they
missed Robin at the station since he had gone home to
Noida looking for them. When they did eventually meet,

Col. Thapar handed over to his son a camera that Robin had always had his eyes on.

'He forgot to load a film though. Robin kept taking pictures with it and realized much later that it had no film. He was so annoyed with his dad,' Mrs Thapar says laughing. 'You should have loaded the film,' she says, looking at her husband.

'There was no time to buy it. He should have checked before using it,' Col. Thapar replies.

Mrs Thapar tells me how Robin's picture appeared in an article published in *India Today* while the war was on. They had bought copies that they kept for him to read when he came back from the war. She says that she had received a call from the magazine's chief photographer, Dilip Banerjee, who said that he had met Robin in the war zone and that her son was a very brave man. Two days later she had received news of Robin's death. She had called Dilip and told him, her voice suffused with sadness, 'My son was a brave man but he is no more.'

A few years later when film director J.P. Dutta was researching for his film *L.O.C. Kargil*, he spoke to Mrs Thapar. 'If it wasn't for you my son would still be alive,' she had told him softly. 'He had seen your film *Border* seventeen times. He was so inspired by the character of Lt Dharam Vir, played by Akshaye Khanna, that he modelled himself after him during the Battle of Tololing and would keep playing the song 'Sandese Aate Hain' in his bunker all the time.' Dutta had included the Battle of Tololing in the film, with Amar Upadhyay playing Vijyant Thapar.

She recounts the phone call that broke her heart forever. 'I was at school when my younger son, Birdie, called me to say that Robin had been martyred in the war. He was at home that day and had received a phone call from the Army headquarters.' Her eyes fill with tears. Col. Thapar quietly looks away. Since there is nothing one can say to console parents who have lost their child, I look away too.

My attention is drawn to a beautiful oil painting of a cheerful-looking red-breasted bird that watches us with its head tilted slightly to a side from their sitting-room wall. 'Our younger daughter-in-law gifted this painting to us on Robin's forty-first birthday. It's a robin,' Mrs Thapar says, smiling bravely despite her moist eyes. Col. Thapar puts an arm around her. If he were around, Robin would probably have been as proud of his parents as they are of him.

————

The battle of Knoll
26 June 1999
Dusk
Dras

A 2 Raj. Rif. convoy is winding its way towards the small hill town of Dras, the second-coldest inhabited place in the world at 10,990 feet.

Dras, however, is not its destination. Just before the Army Mess, there is a left fork in the road. The trucks take that turn and the road gives way to a rough dirt track. Dusk has fallen but no headlights have been switched on. All brake lights have also been disconnected earlier in the morning. The soldiers know that they are in direct line of enemy observation and don't want to alert them about their arrival. The trucks make their way forward slowly in the purple darkness, gravel crunching under their tyres; the silence disturbed only by the rustle of the wind and the soft growl of the engines. The soldiers sitting inside are not in the mood for any kind of conversation either.

The trucks have come all the way from Kupwara, nearly 200 km away, but today they have travelled 20 km from Matiyan, where the unit has been camping. Tololing has been captured at great human loss and the men are now on their way to the next battle. Their task is to evict enemy soldiers lodged in Knoll, a post occupied surreptitiously by Pakistani soldiers in the freezing winter. The soldiers are seated in groups of ten; the officers sit in front, next to the drivers.

Lt Vijyant Thapar and Lt Praveen Tomar, both course mates from the IMA, both twenty-two years old, and barely seven months in the battalion, are seated in different trucks. Both are lost in their own thoughts. One of them will not return alive from the battle. Vijyant, who has been tasked with leading the attack, seems to have pre-empted the possibility that he might be the one. Just a few days ago, he had handed over to Praveen a letter addressed to his family, gruffly saying, 'If I don't come back, please give it to my dad.' A sombre Praveen had nodded and slipped it inside his pocket.

———

The attack
28 June 1999
8 p.m.
Firebase

It is the night Knoll has to be attacked. Temperatures have fallen to below freezing point and the down jackets are coming handy. No one is hungry. No one wants to talk. Every soldier knows that all of them will not return alive but each one wants to believe that death will not come to him.

Wishful thinking and Karni Mata's blessings give the men of 2 Raj. Rif. the courage to move on. The regiment's silver idol of Karni Mata, which dates back to before World War II, has been carried to the battlefield. A quick puja is performed and, with shouts of 'Raja Ram Chandra Ki Jai', the soldiers start lining up for the attack.

Vijyant, 2IC, Alpha Company, is to lead the attack with a platoon of around thirty men. Maj. Padmapani Acharya, Company Commander, Alpha Company, and

Subedar Sunayak are ready to follow with their own sections. Unfortunately, it is a full moon night that makes it easy for the enemy soldiers, sitting in their sanghars on the heights, to observe movement below. Vijyant doesn't know this but his troops have already been spotted and the coordinates conveyed to the enemy artillery guns lined up on the other side. Just as the soldiers gear up for the attack, the first salvo hits them hard.

The silence of the night is punctuated by the noise of artillery fire and the heart-rending cries of men in pain. Screeching shells shatter all around, deafening the soldiers and cutting through them with jagged pieces of shrapnel. Illuminating flares light up the area like daylight and air bursts rain down metal on the hapless soldiers. There is complete mayhem. The men scatter, hiding behind whatever cover they can find, hands covering their ears, the ground shaking beneath their feet.

Vijyant's buddy, Naik Jagmal Singh, is one of the first to be hit. He is devastated by the loss but does not lose his cool. Eyes flashing with determination, he gathers all the able-bodied men he can find in the darkness, regroups his platoon and goes down into the depression to dodge the barrage of artillery fire. His platoon is given up as lost by CO Col. Ravindranath, who orders Acharya and Sunayak to move ahead. Vijyant and his men lose their way in the ensuing chaos but he has no intention of quitting. For the next four hours he and his men go around trying to locate Knoll in the freezing cold with temperatures having dropped to −15 degrees. Breathing is a struggle but the soldiers, carrying 20 kg backpacks, climb the mountains, single-mindedly pursuing their objective. They are destined to join the others in the midst of raging battle.

Losing Maj. Acharya

Maj. Acharya and his men are the first to reach Knoll and make contact with the enemy. Sunayak and Section 1 soon join them. Under Acharya's firm and fearless command, they fight bravely and manage to capture the first of the three sanghars without any casualty.

There is, however, no time to rejoice as deadly fire is coming their way from the other two sanghars, the first of which is just 20 metres ahead and separated by a depression. The two teams retreat behind rocks and start returning fire. The Pakistani soldiers, scathing under their defeat, are directing abuse at them that is making Acharya simmer with anger. He furiously aims his gun at the sanghar ahead, his finger on the trigger.

'*Sahab, cover lo* [Sir, take cover]!' yells Subedar Man Singh, who has seen the swing of a khaki-clad arm on the next sanghar. Acharya turns his head, but it is too late. The grenade explodes right in front of the young officer sending razor-edged shrapnel flying into his chest. The metal pieces cut like knives and Acharya falls. His fingers go limp and he drops the AK-47 by his side. Man Singh screams as pieces of shrapnel cut into his thigh as well and he rolls over towards the gorge, his body disappearing behind a boulder. The unit does not see him and presumes he is dead. He, however, manages to survive.

The message reaches a shocked Lt Col. Ravindranath, who is in constant touch with his men. He orders Subedar Bhupinder Singh to immediately start from the firebase with the fourth section. Using each other for support, the men climb up as quickly as they can. Since the first sanghar has been taken by then, they do not face any opposition and reach quickly. They take position beside their comrades and start firing at the next target.

———

Robin's Story

29 June 1999
1 a.m.
Knoll

It has been nearly five hours since Robin and his men lost their way. They have been wandering on the ridge, confused by its numerous false crests, and are tired, frozen to the bone and itching for a fight. The silver moon that hung silently over their heads when they were climbing has moved behind the ridgeline now. When they hear the sound of gunfire, their faces light up despite their fatigue.

Robin points towards the ridge where the action seems to be taking place.

'That has to be Knoll. Let's go,' he says, pushing his rifle behind his back, and starts climbing the steep rocky incline, pulling himself up with his hands.

The men reach the top to find themselves in the midst of a deadly firefight. Subedar Bhupinder Singh is directing the fire.

'*Acharya Sahab kahan hai* [Where is Maj. Acharya]?' Robin asks.

For a while, the older soldier tries to evade an answer, not wanting the young Vijyant, who is very attached to Acharya, to get a shock in the middle of the battle. After about ten minutes, Vijyant starts getting impatient.

'*Acharya Sahab kahan hain?*' he asks Bhupinder, his voice as cold as the lashing wind.

'*Sahab shaheed ho gaye* [He is no more],' Bhupinder replies quietly.

Tears slip down Vijyant's cheeks. He is inconsolable. Just then Naik Anand, from Vijyant's section, who has been handling the LMG, also gets shot down by an enemy bullet.

Thapar is livid. '*Main aage jaunga* [I will go ahead],' he tells Bhupinder, who is imploring him to stay behind cover.

Holding his AK-47 firmly in his hand, Vijyant moves amidst flying bullets and takes position next to Lance Hav. Tilak Singh. Pushing a magazine into his rifle, he joins the firefight. Under his inspiring leadership, the men are able to dominate the enemy and the second post is also taken.

Vijyant now concentrates on the third position. The enemy sitting there is shooting down at the men of 2 Raj. Rif. who are not being able to step out from behind the cover of boulders. The frustrating status quo remains till around 2 a.m., when the moon climbs higher up in the sky.

Then comes the moment that shall stay frozen in military history forever. Seething with fury from the loss of his beloved company commander and his men, Vijyant changes the course of the battle by stepping out and shooting the enemy soldier handling the LMG. He is shot by the enemy and breathes his last on those freezing heights but his men go on to avenge his death by fighting bravely and taking over Knoll. It happens perfectly in synch with a quote he often used to scrawl in his diary:

'If I lead, follow me
Should I retreat, shoot me
If I die, avenge me.'

Amidst the chaos of the battle and gunfire, Lance Hav. Tilak leans back against the boulder with Robin in his arms and weeps loudly for the young life lost.

He does not realize then that the bullet hasn't killed Robin. It has made him immortal. For times to come, he shall continue to inspire a thousand others. His story will shake up young people lost in the world of video games and YouTube streamings, and inspire them to the join the Army. The songs he has sung will surface as attachments on emails. Girls will find in him their soulmate. Young parents will name their sons after him. The last letter he wrote will be circulated on Instagram and Facebook. His house will become a pilgrimage for those aspiring to join the Army. Young people, dreaming of wearing the uniform, shall walk the roads of Noida, looking for his address. They will locate Vijyant Enclave and ask people for directions to the house where his parents still live. They will stand on their toes and peep over the brick wall to look at the house with the small green lawn where he once laughed and smiled, where Col. Thapar has proudly replaced his own nameplate by his son's—Lt Vijyant Thapar, VrC, of Dras Raj. Rif.

Nineteen years have passed but even now sometimes, when Col. and Mrs Thapar are having tea in their sitting room, and the curtain happens to be drawn, they find curious college kids peeping over the wall. Col. Thapar says his heart fills with pride and Mrs Thapar says that she remembers another summer afternoon, when Robin had come back from college and, after a quick lunch, had dragged Birdie away, saying 'Today, I shall show you an awesome place.' The boys had returned late in the evening. A sullen Birdie had walked into the kitchen to complain to his mother. 'He dragged me all the way to

Param Vir Chakra Lt Arun Khetarpal's house,' he said. 'We didn't even go in. Robin just stood outside the wall and gaped with his mouth open.' Robin, who had just walked into the kitchen, declared loftily, 'I want to be like him one day. People will come to see my house too.' Mrs Thapar had then smiled and got back to rolling out paranthas for dinner.

———

His Story

Robin was born on 26 December 1976 in Naya Nangal, a small town on the banks of the Sutlej on the border of Himachal Pradesh and Punjab. He was one month old and yet to be named when his parents took him to Pathankot where his father was posted. One evening, Maj. Virender Thapar was walking in the cantonment looking absent-mindedly at the Vijayanta tanks parked there when it suddenly struck him that Vijyant, which meant victorious till the end, was a nice name for his son. Mrs Thapar liked the name too and Robin was officially named Vijyant after the main battle tank of the Indian Armoured Corps.

'He was born to join the forces. It was in his heart, his psyche and his blood. And look at the coincidence. He even joined 2 Raj. Rif. that has the motto, "Ever victorious",' Col. Thapar tells me.

Robin grew up in the cantonments of the Indian Army. He was a happy-go-lucky child who would chase butterflies in the garden, pick mock battles with monkeys sitting on the boundary wall, his shimmering black-coated Doberman, Kartoos, running behind him. When he was four, his father commanded 14 J&K Rifles in Barrackpore. There Robin had the best adventures of his life. They lived in an old sprawling bungalow that had ten rooms and massive lawns. Robin made the most of the place, spending his entire day exploring the gardens around the house. 'In the evening, when I would check his pockets before putting his clothes in the laundry, I would come across all kinds of stuff, right from twigs and flowers to crawling ladybirds,' remembers Mrs Thapar. Often, he would go to his dad's battalion, mingle with wrestlers in the *akhada*, who would give him oil massages and share with him walnuts and almonds. At the age of six, he fired his first pistol, holding the shiny Webley & Scott in his pudgy hands while sitting in his father's lap at the firing range.

After completing his tenth standard from St Joseph's, Pathankot, Robin went on to complete grade twelve from DAV College, Chandigarh. When Col. Thapar got posted to Rangia, Assam, Mrs Thapar stayed back in their Noida house to be with the two boys. Robin joined Khalsa College in Delhi to pursue BCom. (Honors). He cleared the CDS exam and, along with his two close friends, went for the SSB to Bhopal.

Col. and Mrs Thapar waited for Robin to call and tell them the result, which they knew would be out by 1 p.m. They knew that out of sixty boys only three were to be selected and were a little nervous.

'When it was nearly 5 p.m. and no call came from Robin, Col. Thapar left the house saying, 'I don't think he has made it.'

Soon after, the phone rang. Mrs Thapar answered it to find Robin on the line. 'I've been selected, Mamma,' he said.

When a delighted Mrs Thapar asked him why he had not called earlier, the eighteen-year-old replied, 'Mamma, both my friends didn't make it. *Woh bahut ro rahe the, main unhe station chorne chala gaya tha* [My friends, who couldn't make it, were crying. I had gone to drop them at the railway station],' Both those friends, Rajesh Makkar and Rahul Joshi, made it in the next attempt and are now serving colonels in the Army.

Mrs Thapar remembers affectionately how Robin was a soft-hearted boy. 'He once gave all his pocket money, a precious sum of Rs 50, to a beggar sitting outside the house. When his father asked him why he had done that he replied, '*Aap ne mujhe pocket money de diya na* [You gave me the pocket money]. Now it is mine. Please let me do what I want with it. I won't ask you for more.'

Always an above-average student, Robin bloomed in the IMA. 'He won prizes for swimming, water polo and debating, and also the silver medal for best runner-up cadet in the first semester,' recollects Mrs Thapar. During his second term at IMA, Robin dislocated his shoulder and ended up with his arm in a sling. He was in great agony but, egged on by Col. Thapar, decided to take part in the final exercise where he had to walk 18 km with a backpack. He managed to complete it and finally, on 12 December 1998, Lt Vijyant Thapar passed out of IMA at the age of twenty-one. Six months later he died fighting in Kargil.

'He joined the IMA at nineteen, became an officer at twenty-one and a martyr at twenty-two,' says Col. Thapar wistfully, looking at Robin's larger-than-life portrait in uniform that covers a wall in the room where he once lived.

Back to the Battle

Tilak lays Vijyant down gently and sets his LMG back into position. He wipes his tear-stained face with the back of his hand and goes back to firing at the enemy. The battle rages till nearly 6 a.m.

Dawn is breaking over Knoll when the firing finally ceases from the enemy side and the Indian soldiers start coming out of cover, their rifles still in their hands, faces tired, sleep-deprived and grief-stricken. Victory has come but at a great cost.

Around 6.30 a.m., a fierce round of screaming enemy artillery shelling rocks Knoll. The enemy is desperate to take back what it has just lost. The rounds, however, cause no damage. Around 9.30 a.m., Subedar Bhupinder breathes a sigh of relief when Maj. Sandip Bajaj, 2IC, arrives with Subedar Ram Chander Lamba and the men of Bravo Company as reinforcements. Bajaj and his men take charge of the captured sanghars and the battle-weary Alpha Company is asked to go back to the firebase.

The jawans use their line bedding to tie up two rifles parallel to each other and cover them with waterproof sheets to form stretchers. The bodies of Maj. Acharya, Lt. Thapar, Naik Anand and Rifleman Jagmal are wrapped in rain capes and placed on these. The weary soldiers carry the makeshift stretchers down over the steep mountainside, taking turns, four at a time.

The battle objective has been met but there is no joy in the hearts of the men or their CO. Memories of the comrades they have lost cloud their eyes. The guns have finally fallen silent at Area Knoll, the Tricolour is flying from the bare grey rocks. Thirteen soldiers lost their lives that night. Twenty-two-year-old Vijyant Thapar is one of them.

Ruksana

One of the most fascinating stories about Lt Vijyant Thapar is of the beautiful bond he had formed with a three-year-old Kashmiri girl while he was posted in the Valley. Robin had first noticed the large-eyed, unusually quiet Muslim girl standing outside a tiny hut in Kandi, Kupwara, when he was there with his battalion, 2 Raj. Rif., fighting insurgency.

While going back and forth on his missions, Vijyant would see her standing outside her small hut, watching the soldiers fearfully. When he inquired about her he was told that she had lost her voice after undergoing the trauma of watching her father, a woodcutter, brutally murdered in front of her eyes by militants a year back. They had suspected him of passing on information to the Indian Army. Deeply moved by her story, the soft-hearted Vijyant would wave and smile at her while going about his duties. When he had time, he would go to her and offer her the chocolates he always carried in his pockets. Slowly he managed to win the child's trust. She started smiling and, much to her mother's surprise, even speaking to the young Army officer. Vijyant started giving Ruksana's mother money for her upkeep and even wrote to his own mother about her.

'He asked me to get some salwar kameez stitched for her, telling me they should fit a three-year-old,'

Mrs Thapar remembers. 'I assured him that I would and he said he would take them back the next time he came home on leave. 'She will be so happy, Mamma,' he had said.'

In the last letter he wrote to his parents from the battlefield, Vijyant had requested Col. Thapar to keep supporting the girl if anything happened to him. Col. Thapar managed to locate Ruksana with a lot of difficulty after Robin was martyred because she had moved with her family. He has not just been visiting her, but also sponsoring her ever since, thus keeping his son's word.

'Ruksana is twenty-two years old now and studying in class twelve,' Col. Thapar tells me. 'I make it a point to meet her every year when I go on my pilgrimage to Dras. I always carry a gift for her and she hands me a box of apples that I bring back to Delhi. Last year, we gave her a computer she had wanted.' Mrs Thapar tells me that they have planned a nice wedding gift for Ruksana whenever she decides to tie the knot. 'That will be for her from Robin,' she says.

Author's Note

For his raw courage, exemplary valour and making the supreme sacrifice while facing the enemy, Lt Vijyant Thapar was posthumously awarded a Vir Chakra. 2 Raj. Rif. lost four officers, two JCOs and seventeen Other Ranks in the war;

70 were wounded, of whom six lost their limbs. It was the first of seven Indian Army units to get a unit citation from the Army chief, recognizing their extraordinary bravery in the Kargil War.

This story is based on conversations with Col. Virender Thapar (retd) and Mrs Tripta Thapar. War scenes have been recreated from the accounts given by Col. Praveen Tomar and Subedar Bhupinder Singh (retd) who was in the final battle with Vijyant and is now a basketball coach with a school in Delhi.

Story 2

Burying the Dead

15 July 1999

It is a biting cold morning when the Army Aviation Corps' small Cheetah helicopters, adept at high-altitude flying, start taking off one at a time from Dras. They are ferrying journalists up to almost 18,000 feet to a location near Point 4875, later renamed Batra Top after young Capt. Vikram Batra, martyred here in a bloody battle barely a week ago. 13 J&K Rifles is organizing a ceremonial burial of seven enemy soldiers, who were killed in the same battle, but whose bodies are not being accepted by the Pakistan Army.

A small ten-by-ten-foot patch of land has been flattened and cleared by the soldiers of Charlie and Delta Companies to create a makeshift helipad. Less than 200 metres away is Point 4875. The operation ended on the morning of 7 July. It was a glorious victory but achieved at a very high price. The battalion has lost five of its brave men, including Capt. Batra who had been promoted on the battlefield at Tololing after an earlier victory. It has also suffered seventeen non-fatal casualties. The injured have been evacuated, the bodies of martyred soldiers have been carried down to Dras, but the bodies of the slain enemy still lay scattered on the battlefield, most dressed in khaki trousers and jerseys with parkas on top.

From the letters and identity cards found, it has become obvious that the slain soldiers are regulars of the Pakistani Army but Pakistan is refusing to accept this and maintains that its Army had no role to play in the infiltration. It has been decided that the dead soldiers shall be buried with due respect. More than thirty soldiers have been killed in battle; some have fallen deep into the ravines but seven bodies have been located, laid out on ground sheets and carried to the burial ground created between Point 4875 and Area Flat Top.

'While we were fighting them, they were our enemies. After death, they were soldiers, just like us, who had died while doing their duty,' says Rifleman Sunil Kumar, SM, of Delta Company, 13 J&K Rifles, remembering the day when he was one of the soldiers carrying bodies and digging graves for them. He says there was no ill feeling towards the dead in the hearts of the soldiers.

He remembers a humorous interaction with enemy soldiers even in the midst of the deadly battle. At one point, when the two armies were fighting each other from barely 15 metres away, a Pakistani soldier taunted, '*Yaar, itni goliyan kyun chala rahe ho. Hume Madhuri Dixit de do, hum wapis chale jaayenge* [Don't waste your ammunition. Just give us Madhuri Dixit and we will go back].'

An Indian soldier retorted, '*Tum Madhuri Dixit ke sapne dekh rahe the, yahan tumhe Dharmendra mil gaye* [While you were dreaming of Madhuri Dixit, you have run into Dharmendra].'

A maulvi has been requisitioned for the burial. Naik Ikraj Nabi, of 16 Grenadiers, had been located in Dras. He trekked nine hours to get to the point, using a stick to navigate the tough climb with four soldiers by his side. Belonging to a village in Rajasthan, Nabi had taken bullets in Doda in 1995 and is happy to be of some help again. He now stands on the flat land in his Army fatigues, trousers flapping in the cold wind, head bound in a thick woollen olive green balaclava, hands in the air, reciting verses from the Quran.

He had earlier instructed the soldiers on how to dig the graves—they had to be in a direction at a right angle to the direction of the Qibla (Mecca) so that the body, placed in the grave lying on its right side, faced the Qibla. Every instruction was followed with complete sincerity. Shovels and pickaxes in hand, black bandanas tied around their heads, the battle-weary soldiers had used all their remaining strength to cut through the rocky mountain. However, the ground was so hard that three and a half feet was the deepest they could go. National flags of Pakistan had been specially stitched in Dras and brought up. Each dead soldier was wrapped in the flag and gently lowered into the shallow grave. The maulvi recited the Salat al-Janazah and the graves were covered.

Besides media representatives, the ceremony is also watched over by Lt Col. (now Lt Gen.) Yogesh Joshi, CO, 13 J&K Rifles, Maj. (now Col.) Vikas Vohra, Company Commander, Delta Company, and soldiers of Charlie and Delta companies who have been part of the battle. 'Today we're carrying out the burial of seven Pakistani soldiers who laid down their lives in combat here as a mark of respect to the soldiers who have died,' Lt Col. Joshi informs the gathered journalists. A rock with the words 'Pak 12 NLI' painted on it is put up at the site. The burial starts around 12 noon and is over by 2 p.m. Thereafter the journalists are again helicopter-lifted and dropped back to Dras, with the choppers doing nearly fifteen sorties late afternoon.

As the sun disappears behind the tall peaks, the sunshine is replaced by freezing cold. The soldiers stand on the barren peak watching the Cheetahs getting smaller and finally disappearing. They then painstakingly mark each grave with a stone and demarcate the entire area by encircling it with stones painted white with the chuna (lime) that was carted up earlier.

It is 3 p.m. by the time they complete their task. The wind has turned chilly and dusk is starting to descend on the valley. The weary soldiers trudge back to cold and desolate

Batra Top, cook themselves some rice and dal from the stocks left behind by the enemy soldiers and take shelter behind boulders. As the temperature dips further, they spread out their sleeping bags and climb into them. The neighbouring features of Whale Back and Twin Bumps have also been captured by 17 Jat and 2 Naga respectively so they aren't tense any more. They watch as the stars come out one by one and night falls silently on Batra Top. Thinking of their families who await their return, hot food and the warm smiles of the ones they love the most, they fall asleep one by one. The vanquished enemy is just 200 metres away, laid to rest forever.

Author's Note

This piece is based on a conversation with Col. Gurpreet Singh, who was Company Commander, Charlie Coy, 13 J&K Rifles, in the war. In the fifty-four days of deployment in the war, the battalion recaptured five heights and won thirty-seven gallantry awards, including two PVCs.

Chapter 5

Premonition

A young officer takes off his engagement ring and leaves it behind before heading out for a battle.

5 July 1999
7 a.m.
Mushkoh Valley

It is a cold, wind-lashed morning. On the barren brown mountain, where temperatures dip to two degree Celsius even in peak summer, Col. Umesh Singh Bawa, CO, 17 Jat, stands facing twenty-three-year-old Capt. Anuj Nayyar of Charlie Company, the icy wind whipping their unwashed hair and sunburnt faces. Anuj has been tasked with leading a platoon to reinforce Delta Company that has wrested the feature Whale Back from the enemy after a fierce battle but is facing ferocious counter-attacks. Maj. Deepak Rampal, Company Commander, D Coy, has sent a desperate message to his CO on the radio set that ammunition has almost run out. Anuj is being sent to his aide.

'An opportunity to go for war comes to the most fortunate soldiers, Anuj,' Col. Bawa tells his young officer, who stands before him, his arms ramrod straight by his side. 'You are lucky it has come to you so early in your life.' Looking into Anuj's eyes, Col. Bawa rests an arm on his shoulder. 'You have a chance to be remembered forever, don't miss it. You can either be brave and have a shot at everlasting glory or fail in your duty and be called a coward for life. This is your chance to create history. Go and make a name for the battalion.'

Anuj's handsome face radiates courage. His young eyes sparkle. They show no fear. But he slips off his engagement ring and takes his wallet out of his pocket. He opens it and looks briefly and tenderly at the picture of his fiancée, a pretty schoolmate he fell in love with at Army Public School, Dhaula Kuan, between bunking classes and playing basketball. She is smiling up at him. He hands both his ring and wallet to his CO. 'Will you please keep these for me, sir?' he asks.

'Wear the ring, Anuj. It will inspire you to fight with even more courage,' Col. Bawa tells him.

However, Anuj is adamant. 'I don't want these to fall into the dirty hands of the enemy. Please keep them,' he says.

Col. Bawa, who too is from Delhi like Anuj and had met the young bride-to-be when Anuj brought her over to his house one evening, gets sentimental. 'Nothing will happen to you, my boy,' he tells Anuj. 'You will come back to us. Go and do your duty. I shall keep your belongings safe.'

Sixth Sense

Talking to me nearly twenty years later, Brig. U.S. Bawa VrC, SM, who has retired and is now settled in Gurugram, says Anuj probably had some kind of premonition about what was to come, but none of them realized it then.

That morning, Anuj led thirty-five men of Charlie Company to Whale Back. He covered the distance from the base camp to the post in just two hours, ensuring that he wasted no time in reaching the soldiers helpless without ammunition. By 10 a.m. he is with his comrades. They find that D Coy has managed to beat back an enemy counter-attack at 8 a.m. but more than thirty enemy soldiers can be seen regrouping for another attack. It comes around 1 p.m. By then ammunition has been distributed LMGs have been loaded and 17 Jat is ready for the enemy. Deepak and Anuj, the two officers, and their men put up a strong fight and the enemy is pushed back. Around 5 p.m. the Pakistanis make one more attempt to take back the post but are defeated again. Finally, night falls and the enemy soldiers retreat. Whale Back has been captured. It is a big

win for the Indian Army but Anuj's moment of glory is yet
to come.

———

The last battle
6 July 1999
8 p.m.
Feature Whale Back

Charlie Company has been tasked with attacking the feature
Pimple 2. Company Commander Maj. Ritesh Kumar is
leading a platoon of around thirty-five men. Anuj is right
behind him. The soldiers have been surviving on man-packs
for two days. They only have shakkarparas, mathis and
stale puris in their backpacks. Anuj is hungry and asks for
something to eat. The soldier with him hands him some
cold puris. '*Yeh mujhse nahi khayi jaayengi, yaar (I can't eat
these, my friend),*' Anuj tells him with a wry smile. He gropes
in his own backpack and pulls out a packet of biscuits,
sharing it with those around. '*Chalein?* (Shall we go?)' he asks
and, slinging his rifle behind his back, starts climbing. Just
800 metres short of the objective the soldiers are spotted by
the enemy who starts shelling them. Maj. Ritesh gets splinter
injuries on his legs. Four other soldiers are also injured.

When this is communicated to Col. Bawa on the radio
set, he asks the injured men to return and get treatment at
the Regimental Aide Post. Col. Bawa speaks to Anuj and

asks him to take charge. As the men move up further they meet stiff resistance. Four machine gun positions on the ridge right in front of them are impeding progress. They go on to neutralize three of these but the fourth continues to stay out of their reach, despite multiple efforts. An exasperated Anuj crawls forward on his arms and knees and manages to throw a grenade inside the loophole of the bunker from where the deadly machine gun is blazing but it continues to spew fire.

Around 5 a.m. on 7 July, Col. Bawa, who has been following the battle on his radio set, loses contact with Anuj's team. Every time he tries to contact the young officer, he is met with a deafening silence. Worried, he orders Maj. Punia, who is stationed at Whale Back as reserve for C Coy, to take thirty men and contact Anuj. Punia leaves immediately. Around 7.30 a.m., he calls Col. Bawa. His voice is heavy with grief. 'Sir, I have very bad news. Anuj is no more,' he says. 'I can see him and four soldiers on the ground.'

A devastated Col. Bawa asks him to retrieve the men. 'Drag them behind cover. Maybe they are alive,' he says desperately.

'No, sir, I can see them clearly. They are dead. The enemy is firing continuously. They are not letting us reach the bodies,' Maj. Punia tells him.

With a heavy heart, Col. Bawa asks him to pull back. 'I don't want to lose more men. The enemy is sitting at a height and has spotted you,' he says.

Col. Bawa decides against launching another attack that night because he realizes that the enemy will be waiting for it. Instead, he keeps bombarding the enemy position through the night, ensuring that the Pakistani soldiers do not get any chance to sleep. The next morning (8 July) he orders an attack in broad daylight, soon after breakfast time, assuming that the enemy soldiers who have been awake all night would have their guard down since they would be expecting the Indians to attack only in the night. Exhibiting extreme courage, two platoons of 17 Jat—led by Maj. Deepak Rampal and Maj. R.K. Singh—climb up from two different directions and manage to reach Pimple 2 undetected around the same time. They launch simultaneous attacks at 1 p.m., surprising the enemy completely. A fierce battle ensues till 4 p.m. and the enemy post is finally captured on the evening of 8 July.

The Price of Victory

17 Jat avenged the deaths of its heroes but there is sadness all around at the big losses they have suffered. The battalion's first task is to retrieve the bodies of its martyred soldiers, including Capt. Anuj Nayyar. Soldiers in Anuj's attack team tell Col. Bawa how bravely he fought. There has been a surprise hero in the battle as well. It is Hav. Kumar Singh, a laid-back, unknown soldier of the unit who had never

Proud parents Dr Narinder K. Kalia and Vijaya Kalia pipping Lt Saurabh Kalia, completely unaware of how short-lived their happiness was going to be.

The author with Lt Saurabh's parents at their Palampur (Himachal Pradesh) residence, flanked by the Dhauladhar range.

Dr Kalia continues to fight a case demanding an internal probe into Lt Saurabh's death after he was tortured and killed in Pakistan's custody.

Mrs Vijaya Kalia with the cheque that Lt Saurabh signed and left behind for her. He died before he could withdraw a single salary.

Maj. Sonam Wangchuk, MVC, with troops of
Ladakh Scouts atop Rock Fall after victory.

Sonam in a lighter moment during the intense
two-hour interview for this book.

The handsome Capt. Haneef-ud-din smiles from a photograph in his mother Mrs Hema Aziz's personal album.

Mrs Aziz assured the then army chief, Gen. V.P. Malik, that she did not want another soldier to risk his life to bring Haneef's body back. She also refused the petrol pump that was offered to her.

Lt Vijyant Thapar in his combat greens.

(Left to right) Lt Vijyant Thapar, VrC, Maj. Vivek Gupta, MVC, and Maj. Padmapani Acharya, MVC, smile from their last picture taken in Vijyant's tent. All three lost their lives in the Kargil War.

Dearest Papa Mama Birdie and Gong,

1. By the time you get this letter I'll be observing you all from the sky enjoying the hospitality of Apsaras.

2. I have no regrets; in fact even if I become a human again I'll join the army and fight for my nation.

3. If you can, please come and see where the Indian army fought for your tomorrow.

4. As far as the unit is concerned the new chaps should be told about this sacrifice. I hope my photo will be kept in the 'A' coy mandir with kasni mata.

5. Whatever organ can be taken, should be done.

6. Contribute some money to orphanage. And keep on giving 50/- Rs to Ruksana per month and meet Yogi Baba.

7. Best of luck to Birdie; never forget this sacrifice of these men. Papa you should feel proud. Mama so should you, meet ____ (I loved her). Maureen forgive me for everything wrong I did.

The heart-wrenching last letter Vijyant wrote to his family from the battlefield.

OK then its time for me to join my clan of the Dirty Dozen. Any arty party has 12 chaps.

Best of luck to you all.

Live life King size. yours

Col. Virender Thapar with Ruksana, the Kashmiri girl whom Vijyant had asked him to take care of in his last letter.

Young cadet Anuj Nayyar at the National Defence Academy.

A proud moment for the Nayyars at Anuj's passing-out parade.

Anuj being promoted to captain on the battlefield.

Anuj after an operation in Kargil.

Capt. B.M. Cariappa flanked by Lance Naik Sher Singh and Naib Subedar Ram Niwas.

Capt. Cariappa and his boys of 5 Para on a peak after a successful operation.

(Left to right) Maj. H.S. Jaggi, Dr Capt. Vikram Grewal (Gary) and
Commanding Officer Col. A.K. Shrivastava of 5 Para taking a breather.

Gary with his patient Hunar Shah, the Pakistani prisoner of war (POW).

Lance Naik Bachan Singh, Lt Hitesh's father, who died during the Kargil War.

Lt Hitesh Kumar with his brother, Hemant, and mother, Mrs Kamesh Bala,
after his passing-out parade.

Mrs T. Angmo Shuno and her son Ricky who did their bit
to support the Indian Army in Leh.

Flight Lieutenant Gunjan Saxena was Kargil's lone woman warrior.

Soldiers of 13 J&K Rifles respectfully buried enemy soldiers killed in battle.

Late Capt. Kernal Sher Khan, whose bravery was
recognized and endorsed by the Indian Army.

Memories of Kargil martyrs sprout from the same soil that they gave up their lives for. These trees that grow in Kannur, Kerala, were planted by an anonymous person or organization.

Mrs Hema Aziz and artist Hutansh Verma with the latter's painting of Capt. Haneef.

The gentle unassuming fighter pilot who went on to bomb Tiger Hill:
Air Marshal Raghu Nambiar.

A painting by Group Captain Deb Gohain depicting the iconic Mirage strike
on Tiger Hill by then Wing Commander Raghu Nambiar and Squadron Leader
Manish Yadav.

done anything remarkable in his career. He was one of the soldiers who had to give promotional cadre exams from havaldar to naib subedar. Just before the unit left for the battle, on 1 July, Col. Bawa had called all the havaldars and told them, 'I am promoting all of you without taking any exams. Now, it is your turn to prove that you are worthy of it. You have to show the battalion that you deserved your promotion. The war is your opportunity to do so.'

Hav. Kumar Singh had fought fearlessly and with extreme courage. He was martyred while clearing the third bunker on Pimple 2.

Anuj had also honoured his CO's wishes. Col. Bawa later learnt that he had led his men with complete disregard for his own life. He had been standing near a boulder, taking respite in a moment of peace in the midst of the battle. He had probably been planning his next move, aware of the fact that the dark sky was slowly turning orange with dawn breaking over the tall barren peaks, and that very little time was left. That was when a rocket-propelled grenade had hit him in the neck. Shocked that death had come to him before he could complete his next task, Anuj had looked up for a second to try and see where the treacherous fire had come from but for the first time he could not get his body to obey his mind. He had fallen to the ground and his eyes had shut forever, leaving unfulfilled his dreams of capturing Pimple 2, of owning a new car he had asked his parents for on his birthday on 28 August, and marriage to his school sweetheart in September. Four other soldiers were also martyred at the same position that morning.

For its outstanding performance in the war, 17 Jat was awarded the Chief of Army Staff commendation on the spot, the Battle Honour Mushkoh and the Theatre Honour Kargil. The battalion received forty-one awards that included a Maha Vir Chakra for Capt. Anuj Nayyar; four Vir Chakras for Col. U.S. Bawa, Maj. Deepak Rampal, Capt. S.B. Ghildiyal and Hav. Kumar Singh; six Sena Medals, twenty Mention in Despatches and ten Commendation Cards. The battalion suffered the highest casualty for a unit in the Kargil war. They lost Capt. Anuj Nayyar, JCO Harphul Singh and thirty-four Other Ranks.

Looking back at the war, twenty years later, this is what Col. Bawa had to say: 'It is the ultimate dream of every soldier to go to war. When we were sent to battle I was excited at the opportunity. I thought I would have stories to tell my grandchildren. But after the war, when I saw the coffins of my boys, when I saw my soldiers maimed and disabled in hospitals, when I met grief-stricken parents who had lost their sons and young girls widowed so early in life, my heart was full of sadness. I never want to see another war in my life. Wars only bring misery. They cannot solve any problems.'

A Grieving Mother

Nearly twenty years after the Kargil War, I met Mrs Meena Nayyar, Anuj's mother, over coffee in Delhi's South Extension. We spent more than an hour together and with great affection and moist eyes she told me about the young son she had lost. When I asked her if she had ever gone to see the war memorial at Kargil, her son's last battlefield, she said she hadn't. 'I never wanted to. There is nothing for me there. My son is gone,' she told me, her voice grief-stricken, and I felt guilty about having asked the question. She smiled, talking about the day Anuj (then a student of Army Public School, Dhaula Kuan) missed his school bus and decided to walk home all the way to Janakpuri, where the Nayyars lived in a joint family. 'He was in grade seven. He didn't know the way but he followed the same route that the bus used to take and reached home,' she said, talking about the son who will always stay twenty-three for her. 'His father and I had gone out for lunch so we didn't even know he had missed the bus. *Aisa hi tha Anuj. Bas apne mann ki karta tha* [That's what Anuj was like. He just followed his heart.]'

She remembered how he had fractured his foot in school and was advised by the doctor to not strain the leg. '*Par woh kahan kisi ki sunta tha* [When did he ever listen to anyone]? He started playing football in school. When I noticed his dirty shirt and scolded him for not listening to the doctor, he just started removing his shirt before playing so that it wouldn't get dirty and I wouldn't find out what he had been up to. When I noticed that his vest stayed dirty, he started playing bare chested; putting on his clothes before returning home.'

One memorable morning, Anuj told his parents that someone special was going to come to see them. Soon after, the doorbell rang and a pretty young girl walked in. It was his schoolmate, the daughter of an Army officer. '*Chhoti si ladki thi par woh toh apna rishta khud hi lekar aa gayi* [She was just a child when she came to see us],' Mrs Nayyar remembered with a gentle smile. 'After she left, we asked Anuj if he was serious about her. He coolly said, "*Tabhi toh aap se milwaya hai* [that's why I have introduced her to you]." His father and I were happy about that too. We had never said no for anything to Anuj. Though sometimes I wish I had said no to him more forcefully when he decided to join the Army.'

Mrs Nayyar remembered how she and Anuj's fiancée ran around getting goodies to send to him with an officer who was flying down to his location at the time of war. 'We bought packs of juices and chips and hastily bound them in a parcel. I added an envelope with some money as shagun for Anuj and another for the young officer who was going to war. Anuj never got to see that parcel because he never came back from that operation,' she said. 'The parcel was returned to us with his coffin, his engagement ring, his watch and wallet.' Mrs Nayyar gave all the jewellery they had collected for Anuj's fiancée to her and helped her parents to convince her to marry someone else. 'She was such a vivacious young girl. I would have never wanted her to suffer all her life.' Some people believe that was the reason why Anuj had left his engagement ring behind though Mrs Nayyar says she doesn't know. 'Some people told me he had some kind of premonition, some told me it is uncomfortable to wear a ring while firing which might be why he left it behind. I really would not know. I just know that he would have wanted her to be happy.'

Young Anuj Nayyar, the boy who was the first in his family to join the Army, ended up becoming one of his school's most famous alumni. He might not have returned from the war but the truth is that soldiers never die on battlefields. They continue to live in the memories of their comrades and their countrymen. And if we look at it that way, Anuj shall also live forever in the hearts of those who love him.

Author's Note

This account has been recreated from conversations with Mrs Meena Nayyar, mother of late Capt. Anuj Nayyar, MVC; and Brig. Umesh Singh Bawa (retd), VrC, SM, who was CO of 17 Jat during the Kargil War. The action led by Capt. Anuj Nayyar resulted in the death of nine enemy soldiers and destruction of three MMGs positions of the enemy. For displaying indomitable grit and determination, motivating his men by personal example and making the supreme sacrifice in the true traditions of the Indian Army, Capt. Anuj Nayyar was awarded the Maha Vir Chakra posthumously.

Story 3

Endorsing the Enemy's Bravery

One of the most heart-warming observations I have made while writing war stories is that soldiers recognize and respect bravery, even if it is the enemy.

A perfect example of this is the case of the late Capt. Karnal Sher Khan of the Pakistan Army, who was martyred at Tiger Hill during the Kargil War. Very few people know that the Indian Army was instrumental in the officer being awarded the Nishan-e-Haider, Pakistan's highest gallantry award, which is equivalent to India's Param Vir Chakra.

In July 1999, Capt. Sher Khan was holding five strategically located posts in the Tiger Hill area, touching a height of 16,700 feet. Looming majestically above all other mountains around, Tiger Hill lies 10 km north of the Srinagar–Kargil–Leh highway and dominates a part of it. Its sharp triangular top is visible from the highway, and one of the major attractions for tourists passing through the area.

In 1999, Capt. Sher Khan's company held all the posts on the feature. It was so well-defended that Gen. V.P. Malik stated in his book, *Kargil—From Surprise to Victory,* that it appeared almost impossible to capture. In May, 8 Sikh had tried an assault that had been repulsed. An attack plan was redrawn in July. The mission was handed over to 18 Grenadiers who had had a rest period after their glorious achievements in Tololing, and to 8 Sikh which was already at the base of Tiger Hill. Both battalions were assisted by a crack team from the High Altitude Warfare School to manoeuvre the seemingly impossible climb up a sheer rock face that was picked as the axis of attack to surprise the enemy.

On the night of 3 July 1999, supported by the concentrated fire of twenty-two artillery batteries, the Ghatak platoon of 18 Grenadiers led by Lt Balwan Singh launched an attack on Tiger Hill. Despite the freezing rain, the men, using ropes, climbed up a nearly vertical rock-face. They managed to surprise the enemy but met with strong resistance at the top. On the night of 5 July, Maj. Ravindra Singh, Lt R.K. Shehrawat and fifty-three soldiers of 8 Sikh launched a daring attack, climbing up from the adjoining Western Ridge. Enemy defences were split up because of their attack. 8 Sikh fought bravely even though most of the Sikh soldiers did not have proper cold-weather clothing and many of the wounded died from the extreme cold and chilling winds. Between 5 and 7 July, intensive fighting went on for control over Tiger Hill. 8 Sikh did not withdraw an inch despite repeated Pakistani counter-attacks. 18 Grenadiers finally captured Tiger Hill top on 8 July.

Lt Balwan Singh, who led the Ghatak Platoon, was later awarded the Maha Vir Chakra, while Grenadier Yogendra Yadav, a scout in the Ghatak Platoon, received the Param Vir Chakra. 8 Sikh lost one officer, four JCOs and thirty jawans in the Battle of Tiger Hill.

In an interview with the *Indian Express*, Brig. (retd) M.P.S. Bawja, Commander, 192 Mountain Brigade, said, 'When the Pakistani counter-attacks were taking place, I was told by one of the 8 Sikh JCOs that a tall, well-built Pakistani in a track suit was motivating his men for repeated assaults and this was causing a problem for them. I immediately said that he was an officer and that he should be neutralized in order to crush the attacks. Let me tell you that our troops were on the verge of being pushed off the top when with one big effort they gave a war cry, charged and killed this Pakistani officer and his companions. Thirty Pakistanis were killed in this fight and the rest retreated, giving us a famous victory. Capt. Karnal Sher Khan fought very well, rallying his men. We must appreciate this. I also told my GOC that the boy fought very bravely.'

Though Capt. Sher Khan was killed, he won the respect of the Indian officers and troops defending Tiger Hill and the adjoining hills. The officers of both 8 Sikh and 18 Grenadiers watched the brave Pakistani officer fighting till the end.

According to an officer of 8 Sikh, 'After a fierce battle, we recovered Tiger Hill on 4 July. For the next four days we were gradually advancing to recover other features—the Helmet, India Gate and Rhino Horn. Soon after the soldiers of 8 Sikh recovered the feature on 7 July around 8 a.m., Capt. Karnal Sher launched a swift counter-attack with just a handful of Pakistani soldiers. It was suicidal for him to do so in broad daylight because we could see his movements. Yet in the highest of military traditions, he launched an attack. It is a disgrace for any army to be evicted from a post and he wanted to save the Pakistani army from that disgrace.'

Such was the ferocity of his attack that 8 Sikh had to be reinforced by a platoon of 18 Grenadiers. The Pakistani counter-attack was beaten back and fifteen of their soldiers were killed. While other Pakistani soldiers tried to run away, Capt. Sher got his men together and inspired them to fight back by leading from the front. The Sikh regiment beat back his assault, killing ten more Pakistani soldiers. Karnal Sher Khan fought till the end and finally fell when a hail of bullets hit him. Even in his last moments his hands were holding his rifle.

The Indian Army wrote to the Pakistani government citing the bravery of the young officer. On the basis of this recommendation, Capt. Karnal Sher Khan was posthumously awarded the Nishan-e-Haider. Captain Sher Khan's brother, Sikandar Sheikh, has been quoted as saying, '*Allah ka shukar hai ki humara dushman bhi koi busdil dushman nahi hai. Agar log kahen ki India busdil hai to main kahunga nahi kyunki usne aelania keh diya ki Karnal Sher hero hai* [Our enemy is not a coward. I won't call India cowardly because it openly proclaimed Sher Khan as a hero].'

Initially the Pakistan Army did not want to accept that Capt. Karnal Sher Khan had died fighting on the Indian side of the LoC. It was awkward for them to explain how his body was with the Indian Army when they had maintained all along that the Pakistan Army was not involved in the Kargil intrusions. The young captain's body was taken to Delhi and Pakistan was asked to send his relatives to identify him; they refused, asking India to send the body to Pakistan for identification.

Two weeks later, the brave young officer's body was handed over to the International Committee of the Red Cross. Finally, his coffin, draped in the Pakistani national flag, was flown to Islamabad. It was only after three months that Pakistan Army Chief Gen. Pervez Musharraf conceded that Capt. Karnal Sher Khan had indeed died in Kargil. At a ceremony to pay homage to soldiers who died in Kargil, Musharraf said that Sher Khan had 'killed fifteen soldiers' and was in an 'offensive defensive'.

An Officer since Birth

Captain Karnal Sher Khan (1970–99) was born in Naway Kiley (New Village) in Swabi district of Pakistan. It is said that his family was so keen that he join the Army and achieve the rank of colonel that they named him Karnal (a localized version of colonel).

Karnal was the youngest of four siblings and only eight years old when he lost his mother. He grew up to join the Pakistan Military Academy, Kakul, in November 1992 and graduated in 1994. He was a captain in 27 Sindh Regiment of the Pakistan Army and was posted to 12 Northern Light Infantry (NLI) Regiment during the Kargil conflict. He had the reputation of being a proud Pakistani and a very brave officer. In the Battle of Tiger Hill, he proved it even to the enemy.

For his bravery in battle, Pakistan conferred on him the Nishan-e-Haider, its highest gallantry award. Sher Khan's village was renamed Karnal Sher Kally (the village of Karnal Sher). An Army parade ground and a school have also been named after him in Pakistan.

Author's Note

The first week of July 1999 saw three brave young officers, who had the best years of their life in front of them, dying for their nations. On 5 July, Pakistan lost twenty-nine-year-old Capt. Karnal Sher Khan of 12 NLI at Tiger Hill. On 7 July, the

Indian Army lost twenty-four-year-old Capt. Vikram Batra of 13 J&K Rifles and twenty-three-year-old Capt. Anuj Nayyar of 17 Jat in the Mushkoh Valley. All three were recommended for the highest gallantry awards of their country. While Capt. Sher Khan and Capt. Vikram Batra were awarded the Nishan-e-Haider and the Param Vir Chakra respectively, Capt. Anuj Nayyar was decorated with the Maha Vir Chakra.

Chapter 6

Endgame

*O*n the barren heights of Batalik, fourteen paratroopers
are surrounded by the enemy and are left with
no choice but to ask for Bofors' fire upon their own
coordinates.

21 July 1999
Muntho Dhalo

The sun is setting on the hills of Batalik. Lean and sinewy,
Carie sits crouched behind a boulder, his weight on his
haunches, gun firmly clasped in his hands, his face a
scowling mask. Up ahead, in the fading orange glow of
dusk, he can see the blurred outline of Area Conical.
Carie fixes his unblinking gaze on the rocky spur of the

mountain. If he stays alive, that is where he should be the next morning, he tells himself.

He has been lucky so far. Not only did he survive enemy bullets in Siachen, but he also returned victorious from an earlier attack on Point 5203. In fact, many of the soldiers with him tonight have volunteered to come along on the near-suicidal mission because they believe they will return alive if he leads them.

Shivering involuntarily as a blast of icy wind hits his exposed face, Carie wishes he could share their confidence. The sun sinks behind the mountains, dropping a sheet of impenetrable darkness over everything. Carie's eyes take a few minutes to adjust. He checks his phosphorescent watch. It blinks a green 1900 hours at him.

'Time to go,' he announces curtly, 'Area Conical waits for us.' His voice permeates the eerie stillness of the night. Each of his men hears it clearly.

Stepping under the open sky, Capt. B.M. Cariappa (Carie) jams a magazine into his INSAS rifle and, slinging it behind his back, starts to walk. He is followed by the ghostly figures of the faithful men of Alpha Company, 5 Para, all ninety-four of them emerging out of the shadows one by one.

Two Hours Later

Carie and his team reach the base from where the tricky climb begins. The night is colder now. When Carie holds his face up, he feels the soft caress of snowflakes on his wind-lashed cheeks. He knows that up on the mountaintops the snow has hardened into razor-edged cornices of ice, grey with cordite from the constant shelling. If these dislodge and fall on a man, they can slice him into pieces.

Running a weary hand across his face to wipe away the beads of sweat that have appeared in spite of the chill, Carie lets it linger on the unruly stubble on his face. His hair is growing back after the tonsure he got after his mother's death a month ago. It pricks his fingers when he feels his head. Like his comrades, Carie has been wearing the same clothes for nearly a month. They have dumped their bulletproof jackets and helmets that would have added to body weight while climbing. His combat uniform is soiled with mud, ripped in places by the sharp rocks he has been crawling over and stained with blood that has spilled and dried many times over.

The war has given him a gift though. It has blurred the pain of his mother's death. Carie had thought he would never get over the haunting memories of her last days in Bangalore where he had sat by her bedside, watching her die a slow, agonizing death from oral cancer. His beautiful mother, with tender loving eyes, had been reduced to a heap of bones and skin, shrivelled between the bed sheets. For many days after he lost her, Carie had recurring nightmares of holding his emotionally shattered naval-officer father in his arms. He had thought the pain would never pass. Carie is surprised to note that in the past two days, he has not thought about her even once. Self-preservation is such a dominating animal instinct, he tells himself, grimacing in the darkness. All that he can think about these days is how to stay alive.

The climb begins. Carie stands still, like a wild animal, trying to sense the men he cannot see. He knows they are around him. He knows, just as they all do, that for some, this will be the last journey of their lives. Like a cat, his eyes adjust to the darkness and he catches a shadowy figure standing a little way off, snow falling around him. Carie tightens his hold on his gun but then his face breaks into a slow smile. The tall, lanky Khalsa standing a little ahead is Maj. Harinder Singh Jaggi, also from 5 Para, who is leading Delta Company on a simultaneous operation that night. While Carie and his company have been tasked to attack Area Conical, Jaggi and his men have been ordered to go through the valley and attack Area Ring Contour, a feature further to its east.

Jaggi has let his column move on and is waiting for Carie's team to catch up. '*Ik vaar jappi te paa le* [Give me a last hug],' he whispers, spreading out his arms. The two friends—dirty, dishevelled, weak from a frugal diet, on a mission where the odds are against them—hold each other close and, wishing each other luck, go in their respective directions.

Carie has split up his men into two columns. While 2nd Lt Vaibhav Dixit, the young officer with him, separates to lead the larger column of seventy up on the raised spur, Carie is taking twenty-four men through the bowl of the mountain. All teams are expected to reach the top before dawn and attack the enemy before sunrise. They have no idea how many enemy soldiers man those posts and what kind of arms and ammunition they have at their disposal. If they start rolling rocks at the climbing columns, the repercussions could be deadly. Only stealth can save their lives.

The climbing soldiers make no noise, they don't use any lights, and they have been told not to step on bare soil. In the past few days, while they camped at Muntho Dhalo waiting for attack orders, they had watched the Pakistanis come down and mine the area.

'We should have bombed the fuckin' bastards right then,' Carie thinks aloud. '*Pathar se pathar per kudo; zameen par paon nahi rakhna hai* [Jump from boulder to boulder, don't step on the ground],' he calls out to his men tersely, slipping his calloused hand into his trouser pocket. His fingers tighten around a small bundle—two bullets tied up in a handkerchief. Every man in his team is carrying two bullets separately, their passport to an easier death. They have heard about the brutally mutilated bodies of Indian soldiers who have been taken prisoners of war (POW) and tortured and have decided that they will not let that happen again. If they run out of ammunition and capture is unavoidable, they plan to use the bullets on themselves.

For a fleeting moment Carie's mind takes him back to the Army trucks he had crossed on his way to Batalik when the war started. He had made his jeep driver stop and asked why the trucks headed for the Leh airfield bore black flags.

'*Sahab, shaheed sipahiyon ke bodies le ke jaa rahe hain* [Sir, we are taking the bodies of our martyrs],' the young driver had told him grimly.

Carie had removed his combat cap as a mark of respect and asked his driver to move on.

———

Day 2
22 July 1999
2.30 a.m.

The soldiers have been climbing for hours. It is freezing cold, but if he lowers his head Carie can breathe in the sickly sweet smell of his own sweat. The stench of his dirty body used to be nauseating till a few days back but he realizes he has become used to it. Just like he has become accustomed to hunger, the searing pain in his left heel where his boot rubs against the scraped heel every time he walks, and the constant threat of death. The INSAS rifle he grips tight in his weather-beaten hands is almost a part of his body now, kept aside only when he has to relieve himself. He passes blood and mucous since there is hardly anything left in his stomach. He knows that most of the men with him are suffering from the same blood dysentery brought on by the stale puris they carry in their backpacks, the cordite-laced ice they suck on to quench their thirst and the suffocating fear of dying so far away from loved ones.

Walking on boulders has been tough. Often the men climb up and then come across a patch of naked land. They then have to retrace their steps and find another rocky route to move over. Unless it is completely unavoidable, they don't risk stepping on land that can have mines that can explode under their feet.

Carie is wondering just how long their luck will last when a loud explosion and the heart-wrenching cries of men in extreme pain pierce the silence of the night. Someone from Jaggi's team has stepped on a mine. The enemy soldiers sitting on top of the feature hear the screams as well. All hell breaks loose as the enemy's air defence guns, mortars and small arms' fire rain down on the ill-fated soldiers.

The Pakistanis haven't realized that Carie and his column are also climbing up from another axis. But, just then, a large boulder dislodged by the shelling comes tumbling down, misses Carie by a whisker and falls on the artillery surveyor below him. The surveyor's screams ring out in the dark. The soldiers freeze, expecting enemy fire. When there is no response from the top, they realize that the screams were not heard in the ongoing firing. The men run down and find the surveyor buried under a seven-foot-high boulder. Fearing the worst they push the boulder down the slope and are relieved to find that he has fallen into a cavity between two rocks and is safe. Other than a deep gash across his nose that has left a fold of skin hanging from his face, he is fine. He is given first aid and the soldiers start climbing again.

———————

4 a.m.
Area Conical

Gripping sharp-edged rocks and continuing to pull himself up, Carie suddenly hears the radio set buzzing. It is Dixit, who has taken the other column of soldiers.

'Bravo to Alpha, Bravo to Alpha,' Dixit's raspy voice comes through.

'Sona. Repeat Sona,' he says.

The men stop in their tracks. Smiles of disbelief run across their faces. 'Sona', which means gold, is their agreed code for victory over Area Conical.

'How many enemy soldiers there?' Carie asks.

'None,' Dixit replies and the radio set goes dead.

Carie finds it strange that the Pakistanis have vacated their post. He tells his men that they might have moved to reinforce the area where Jaggi's column is headed. Some of the tension eases off and the soldiers started climbing up the last stretch, relaxed for the first time in many days.

Finally, Area Conical

It starts snowing again when the men reach the top. Something does not seem right to Carie. He cannot spot any of the seventy men from Dixit's team. He is still observing the area clinically, his eyes moving from left to right, when paratrooper Vikram draws his attention to a man in a sleeping bag lying behind a rough man-made stone wall about 40 feet away.

Assuming it is one of Dixit's men, Carie yells at him, 'The battle is not over yet, you ass, you are supposed to take defences, not sleep.'

The man wakes up lazily and fixes a puzzled gaze on him. Just then another man runs across. He is in khaki trousers, jersey and a balaclava. '*Sahab, ye toh Pakistani hain* [Sir, they are Pakistanis],' Vikram whispers hoarsely.

Carie cocks his gun almost immediately. 'You take the one in the sleeping bag, I'll take the other one,' he shouts, spraying the standing man with a round of bullets. Vikram directs a spray of fire at the other soldier, leaving him dead as well.

All hell breaks loose as the Pakistanis find that they have been ambushed. The area rings out with the noise of rocket-propelled grenades and mortar fire that comes from behind the mountain and leaves the Indian soldiers leaping for cover. Carie realizes that Dixit's party has mistaken a false crest in the mountain for the peak and is lost somewhere below. He radios his CO, Col. A.K. Shrivastava, asking him not to move Dixit's team up since they will get caught in the crossfire. He asks his men to take cover, watch out for gunfire and return it whenever possible.

'*Lance Naik Hemcharan ko goli lag gayi hai,*' a scream rings out. Tall and broad-shouldered with rippling muscles, Ḥemcharan is one of the toughest guys in the team who single-handedly carried the 30 kg medium machine gun over his shoulder. Sweating under its killing weight but insisting that no one else is as strong as him, he has been the backbone of the team.

Carie is shaken to find Hemcharan's body quivering on the ground, his skull caved in from being hit by mortar fire. A shocked Naik Sunil rushes to the fallen soldier with his first-aid kit. Carie screams at him to stop but his warning comes too late. Sunil hasn't even reached his dying comrade when he gets shot multiple times in the chest and falls into a gaping 700-foot gorge. He is swallowed by the darkness even as his comrades watch helplessly. They are both dead but there is no time to grieve.

Carie wipes his moist eyes with the back of his calloused hand and, pushing another magazine into his rifle, gets down to returning enemy fire.

———

9 a.m.

The soldiers have figured out that there is a big enemy camp behind the slope. Someone from there is directing deadly rocket-propelled grenade fire at them very accurately.

Since small arms are no match for it, a frustrated Carie picks up a rocket launcher. He knows only too well that the Carl Gustav Rocket Launcher (RL) has a back blast of up to 15 metres, which means that if there is any obstruction within 15 metres of the rear of the rocket launcher, the back blast could kill or injure the firer. It hasn't been used so far because of the huge rocks behind which the soldiers are taking cover. Carie decides to move out into the open to fire it.

Paratrooper Namdev Pawar tries to convince Carie not to expose himself to the enemy, but he does not listen. Suddenly bombs explode around him and Pawar yells, 'Sahab, aapke sar se khoon beh raha hai [Sir, you are bleeding from a head wound].'

Carie has been hit in the head by metal shrapnel. He is lucky to be alive. The men quickly pull him back, remove the pieces and bandage him as best as they can. Col. Shrivastava is shocked to learn of Carie's injuries and asks him to de-induct while it is still daytime. A bleeding Carie refuses outright, tell him that vacating the position would make the sacrifices of the two men they have already lost worthless since the enemy would move back in.

A furious Col. Shrivastava shouts at Carie, telling him he has already lost Maj. K.A. Somaiah (another Coorgi officer) and does not want to lose one more.

Carie switches off his radio set.

10.30 a.m.

'*Sahab, counter-attack aa raha hai. Dushman ke sipahi humari taraf badh rahe hain,*' [Sir, there is a counter-attack. Enemy soldiers are heading towards us!' yells paratrooper Naresh, who sits overlooking the ridge, operating the LMG.

Carie's heart goes cold. 'How many are there?' he asks.

'*Bahut saare hain, Sahab. Ginti nahi ho rahi . . .* [I can't count how many . . .],' Naresh hasn't even finished speaking when a bullet goes through his mouth, smashes his jaw and makes him keel over and drop down.

With Hemcharan and Sunil gone, Naresh grievously injured and the enemy firing from just 40 metres away, someone is desperately required to handle the LMG. Even as Carie watches spellbound, the broad-shouldered, towering Naik Yudhbir Singh emerges like a colossus from amidst the smoke and rubble. With his rifle behind his back, he is climbing on to the rock where the LMG is positioned. He just manages to reach the gun when a burst of machine gun fire hits him in the arm, reducing it to a bloody mass of flesh.

Carie can see his bare bone jutting out of the wound. But like a superhuman who feels no pain, Yudhbir opens the buttons of his shirt and, using it like a sling, pushes his useless arm inside. He then cocks the machine gun with his good hand and starts firing at the enemy.

Carie leans back, sweating profusely. He realizes he has finished two out of his five magazines and wonders how much longer his team's ammunition will last. '*Goli kam hain, waste mat karo* [We don't have spare bullets, don't waste them],' he calls out, his voice thick with worry.

Bright daylight has flooded the area. Carie can see the approaching Pakistani soldiers clearly now. They are close enough for him to make out that they are in white snowsuits and holding rifles and rocket launchers. Out of his twenty-three men, six have had splinter injuries, one has been shot through the mouth, one has fallen into the ravine and one has been killed by mortar fire. There are just fourteen left and their ammunition is finishing fast.

Just then Naik Kaman Singh comes up to Carie and whispers, '*Sahab, main 500 rounds extra le ke aaya hun* [Sir, I am carrying 500 extra rounds].

Carie wants to hug him in relief but he just nods and asks him to distribute these amongst the able-bodied men. He knows, however, that even these rounds will not last long. The time has come to take a cold, calculated decision for the greater common good.

His mind made up, Carie moves towards to the young artillery officer accompanying his team, who is leaning back on a rock, rifle in hand. 'The enemy is almost upon us, buddy. We are completely outnumbered. There is no choice but to ask for artillery fire upon our own position,' Carie tells him, placing a hand on his shoulder.

The young officer, barely in his twenties, sits down, shivering in the cold, the freezing wind lashing his body. He drops his rifle.

'We are going to die, sir,' he whispers, 'We are all going to die.'

'Let's make sure they die with us then. Call for fire,' Carie says, clearly and calmly. The artillery officer, who has been running high fever, breaks down completely.

Carie shakes him roughly and slaps him hard. 'Snap out of it, man,' he shouts, but the young officer just sits there staring into the distance, tears streaming down his cheeks.

Carie lowers himself next to him, puts his weapon down and, taking the radio set, switches it on. The set crackles and Maj. Gurpreet Madhok, the BC-OP (Battery Commander-Observation Post) comes on the line. He is sitting in Muntho Dhalo from where he can see Area Conical. His job is to direct artillery fire when required.

'The enemy is just 40 metres away from us, we are outnumbered and running out of ammunition; we need fire upon our own coordinates,' Carie tells him.

'Think again, bugger!' Gurpreet answers, his voice hoarse. 'You are asking for fire upon yourself. Bofors is a medium artillery gun with a killing range of 300 metres. The splinters will go flying in all directions. Chances are that you guys will not survive either.'

'We will not survive in any case, sir. We have run out of ammunition. I need the bloody fire here, right now.

They will be upon us in minutes,' Carie shouts in desperation, making his voice heard above the gun battle going on around him. 'These are our coordinates, sir. Refer the centre of the saddle, as you see it, left 100 metres, get whatever you can.'

'Roger! Fire shall be upon you in minutes. Take cover if you can,' Gurpreet answers. 'God bless you,' he adds softly, his voice sad.

Code Red upon Red

Carie tells his men to stop firing. The soldiers retreat behind boulders. Covering their ears with cupped hands, they sit down and wait. Some close their eyes and say their prayers. Others remember parents and children, wives and lovers, and wonder if they will ever see them again.

Except for the sound of the cold wind whipping against hard rock, there is eerie silence on the mountains. The Pakistanis are puzzled why the fire has stopped but they keep advancing; probably presuming that the Indians have run out of ammunition. The seconds tick by so slowly that to the men of 5 Para it seems like years passing.

And then the Bofors guns—lined up on the road near village Dah, 18 km away—come alive. The sky blazes with flashing streaks of fire as they start booming. Screaming shells start falling all around as they rain vengeance on the mountain. Rounds fall just 15 metres away from where

Carie and his men have taken cover. The noise is so deafening that most of them lose hearing temporarily.

The enemy soldiers in the open are taken completely unawares. They start falling like wax statues, melting in the heat of the devastating fire, their cries of pain drowned in the noise of the screaming shells falling on them.

Meanwhile, 2 km away in Muntho Dhalo, Gurpreet sits with his binoculars trained on Area Conical. He is meticulously keeping track of where the rounds are falling, making minor adjustments to correct the range and trying his best to keep them away from his own men. The fire continues from 11 a.m. to 12 noon.

Carie and his men, who sit crouched on the mountain, have experienced enemy rounds falling around them earlier in Siachen. The deafening noise, the ground shaking under their feet, the whistling in their ears as if someone had hit them hard on both sides of the head is familiar. Mentally prepared to die, they know that nothing worse can happen to them now. They lose their fear of small-arms fire completely.

In the gap between salvos, they load their rifles and using single shots to target the enemy soldiers who survive the Bofors shelling. They step out from behind cover and without a care stand exposed in the sunlight; taking aim at the Pakistanis just 15 yards away, they shoot to kill. When the next salvo comes, they leap behind rocks and cover their ears again.

Lanky cross-country runner Basti Ram Bishnoi is spewing filthy expletives as if his swear-word vocabulary is being tested; Subedar Darwan Singh, a fit and ferocious JCO with a bushy black upturned moustache, is laughing loudly as if someone has just told him a joke and Carie stands with a crazy leering half-smile on his face. When the artillery fire finally stops, there is sinister calm on the mountain. And then, the soldiers of 5 Para start stepping out of cover one by one.

Carie cannot believe that all fourteen of them have survived. Fraught with emotion, he goes up to each man and hugs him saying, '*Saale, tu bhi bach gaya* [You are alive too, buddy]!'

The paratroopers stand on the ridge looking in sheer disbelief at the devastating casualties on the Pakistani side. More than twenty-three bodies lie scattered on the slope in front of them. The enemy soldiers are dead, their khaki pants and pathani suits covered in blood and grime. These are men of the 33 Frontier Force.

Return to Dah

The men flop down in sheer exhaustion. They have not slept for two nights. No one has the energy to talk. The soldiers spend the rest of the day and that night firing at Pakistani soldiers who have a camp behind the ridgeline from where they are seen climbing down to their own side. The ferocious artillery fire has broken the enemy's spirit. By 8.30 p.m. Dixit's column comes up. Ammunition is immediately redistributed and positions are taken.

Around 10.30 p.m. the enemy launches a counter-attack. But this time, with more men and adequate ammunition, the counter-attack is thwarted.

In between, the radio set buzzes. Col. Shrivastava comes on line. He is relieved to find that his men are safe. '*Shabash* [Well done]! We are sending another team to replace you. Start de-induction. I am proud of you,' he says, his voice soaked in emotion.

———

Day 3

Daylight is breaking when Carie asks Yudhbir, whose arm is hanging in a tangled mess of skin and stained bandages, to leave for Muntho Dhalo.

Yudhbir refuses point black. '*Chot toh aapko bhi lagi hai, sahab, dard toh aapko bhi ho raha hoga* [You are also hurt, sir, you are also suffering]. If you can tolerate the pain, so can I,' he says.

The bandages around Carie's head are seeped in blood.

'*Theek hai, sath jaayenge* [All right, we shall go together],' Carie tells him.

The de-induction starts with the able-bodied carrying the bodies of their dead comrades. They are followed by the injured, who go down slowly in buddy pairs, helping each other over the steep mountainside. Carie and Yudhbir give each other their shoulders and slowly make their way down.

Extreme exhaustion makes the soldiers falter in their steps. The cordite-laced ice that they have sucked on to quench their thirst is now causing severe stomach cramps. Often, they topple or miss a footstep, but they look out for rocks to place their tired feet on, taking care not to step on the ground. They reach a pool of murky brown water that has collected from melting snow and fall upon it like dogs, lapping it up with their tongues. Finally they tumble down to Muntho Dhalo, falling clumsily into the arms of their comrades who have run across to carry them back.

Carie sees Jaggi lying on the ground with six other injured soldiers. He is relieved to know that they are alive. His energy sapped completely, Carie then collapses.

———

Nineteen years later
May 2018
Beverly Park Apartments
Dwarka, Delhi

The doorbell rings. Huzoor, our beautiful golden retriever scampers across and takes deep breaths in an effort to smell the visitor, one of his favourite pastimes. He is wagging his tail even before I open the door.

I find a distinguished-looking Col. B.M. Cariappa, VrC, SM, standing at the door in a crisp shirt and jeans, grinning widely, holding a big box of cookies. Since he and my brother have been in the war together, he calls himself my brother from another mother. A round of hugs and backslapping later, and after having shaken paws with Huzoor, he sits down at the dining table with the entire family around him. With his legs stretched out comfortably under the table, a mug of chilled beer resting in front of him, Carie sketches clear maps on sheets of paper. He then tells us the story of the war that he was fortunate enough to return from. He has since commanded 5 Para, and is now on his way to serve in the Brigade at Batalik. He has asked to be posted back to the same place where he and his brave soldiers fought for their country nineteen years ago.

Story over, Carie raises his beer mug to his lips. We reminisce about a similar incident from World War II when on 26 December 1944, twenty-nine-year-old Lt John Robert Fox (an American) had realized his position was being overrun by enemy troops and had called for artillery fire on himself. During a counter-attack later, US troops found the lieutenant's body along with those of about a 100 German soldiers. He had not survived.

When I marvel at the narrow escape he and his men had, Carie has a half smile on his lips. 'The bombs fell just

10 metres away from us. When I tell artillery officers my story, they don't believe it. "That was Code Red on Red, bugger. No one survives an attack like that," they tell me. But we did,' he says softly.

There is a faraway look in his eyes. I know he has gone back to that chilly wind-lashed day on Area Conical when the bombs fell around him and his men. I leave him alone with his memories and get busy laying the table for lunch.

A Case of Mistaken Identity

With a wide grin on his face and a twinkle in his eye, Carie likes to recount an amusing incident that happened in the midst of the war. On 24 June 1999, the day after he stumbled back to Muntho Dhalo after the fierce battle, Carie says he woke up to find his head bandaged. He was told that Jaggi and the injured soldiers had been evacuated to a field hospital while Maj. Sameer Anukul and his men had taken over Area Conical. When Carie stepped out of his tent, the first thing he saw was a Pakistani soldier who had been taken prisoner of war.

'He was standing there sipping on a drink from a tetrapak with a straw. In complete contrast to how the Pakistanis had treated our men, he was being taken very good care of. It made my blood boil.'

Soon after, an Army helicopter landed at Muntho Dhalo. It had brought Brig. Devinder Singh, Commander, 70 Brigade, who was also a paratrooper. He had come to meet the victorious troops and then take the POW back with him in the chopper. When he saw the injured Carie, he congratulated him on a job well done and asked him to come along in the helicopter, saying the POW could come later.

Carie, still in his torn combats; his head covered in bandages, went and sat inside the helicopter. The pilot turned around and mistaking Carie for the Pakistani POW shook his fist at him. 'He started hurling the choicest of abuses at me,' Carie smiles. 'I was too tired to correct him.'

Soon after, Brig. Devinder walked in and the chopper took off, landing at Dah in 15 minutes. 5 Para troops had already collected at the helipad, having heard that a chopper was bringing Carie.

'On landing, Brig. Devinder signalled a thumbs at me and left. As soon as I got out of the chopper, I was mobbed by the soldiers who fell upon me affectionately,' he recounts. The Army Aviation Corps pilots could not hear anything over the noise of the rotors and, still under the impression that they had fetched a POW, assumed that the soldiers were beating him up. They leaned out of the helicopter and shouted, '*Chorna nahi isko. Saale ka band bajana* [Don't let him get away. Hit him hard],' and took off.

Once the soldiers had poured their affection on him, Carie was taken to the medical inspection room. Nursing assistants painstakingly pulled out the pieces of shrapnel embedded deep in his head.

The next day, then defence minister George Fernandes landed there. Carie went to meet him in the same tattered battle fatigues. 'Sir, I am Capt. Cariappa from 5 Para,' he said introducing himself.

GOC Gen. V.S. Budhwar was quick to add, 'Sir, he is the tiger of Batalik.'

'*Tu theek toh hai, bete* [Are you all right, son]?' Fernandes asked him, putting an arm around his shoulders.

That evening Carie finally got to speak to his worried father, who had received a message that Carie had received multiple gunshot wounds. He said, 'Dad, I'm perfectly all right.'

Carie's relieved sixty-three-year-old dad could only mumble softly, 'Thank God.'

Author's Note

For displaying bold leadership, unparalleled courage and devotion beyond the call duty in the face of enemy, (then)

Capt. B.M. Cariappa was awarded the Vir Chakra. Hav. Yudhbir was awarded a Sena Medal for his gallant action.

   Then Maj. Gurpreet Madhok is now a serving brigadier. N.K. Namdev Dagdu Pawar was martyred in another operation soon after the Kargil War.

Chapter 7

The Doctor with a Maroon Beret

'*No man who comes to me alive will be allowed to die*', a young doctor promises his comrades on the battlefield.

22 June 1999
7 a.m.
Area Boulders, Muntho Dhalo
Batalik Sector

'Whopwhopwhopwhop . . .'

A new but familiar sound breaks the monotony of gunfire for the battle-weary paratroopers taking cover from enemy shelling behind the massive rocks. As always, they hear the choppers before they see them.

Twenty-six-year-old paratrooper Dr Capt. Vikram Grewal (Gary), his eyes bloodshot from lack of sleep, a dark stubble covering his wind-scarred face, sits leaning against a boulder, one hand clasped tightly around a bottle of saline water. Before him lies his heavily sedated Sikh comrade Maj. H.S. Jaggi, eyes shut, breath coming out in uneven gasps.

Gary is watching the fluid enter Jaggi's vein at the wrist, drop by drop, through the intracath venflo he had pushed in last night. For a moment his gaze lingers gently on Jaggi's lean face and he remembers the countless evenings they have spent on the basketball court in Agra, playing matches with the men. Then, involuntarily, it goes down to the stump where Jaggi's foot used to be. It is wrapped in a blood-soaked bandage. Jaggi's loud cries at midnight, when he had been brought down from the mountain on a soldier's back, after stepping on a landmine, still echo in his ears.

'Kill me, doc. End this suffering!' Jaggi had screamed, 'I want to die.' Quick injections of the potent analgesic Fortwin and a heavy dose of antibiotics had quietened Jaggi but his contorted face and restless slumber told the doctor that he was still in great pain.

'Jaggi Sir, please, please stay alive,' Gary whispers desperately, his eyes moist with tears. The staccato blade-slapping of the helicopters is louder now. He looks down into the barren valley where two tiny black specks are getting larger by the moment. '*Waheguru*,' he mumbles under his breath.

———

'*Doctor Sahab, helicopter aa gaye hain* [The helicopters are here],' whispers twenty-five-year-old paratrooper Parimal Singh, Gary's nursing assistant, a smile of relief spreading across his fatigued face. Parimal is monitoring saline for a soldier from 2 Vikas, who has both his arms, now stumps, tightly wound up in bandages. Half of the soldier's face is gone too, making it look like a macabre mask. He had been a handsome man till he absent-mindedly picked up a Bofors minelet round that had fallen in Muntho Dhalo. Not realizing what it was, he had started twirling it around like a yo-yo. Before the horrified men watching him could scream out a warning, it had blown up in his face.

The disfigured soldier, who had been screaming in unbearable agony till a few hours ago, is silent now. His irregular breathing is the only sign that he is alive. Gary knows only too well that both his critical patients have a chance to live only if the helicopters are able to take them to the Forward Surgical Centre at Batalik in time. He mumbles a silent prayer for the daredevil Army Aviation pilots who are braving enemy fire for casualty evacuation.

The enemy soldiers have heard the choppers as well. The battle still rages on the heights of Area Conical and Ring Contour. A slew of airbursts erupt above Gary's head; their eerie whistle interrupting the staccato gunfire that his ears have become used to. Gary realizes they are trying to bring the choppers down. The two Cheetahs hover uncertainly. The pilots know that one freak hit can send the machines crashing into the bottomless gorge. Gary fears that they will turn and go back. But after a moment of hesitation, the choppers start to move forward determinedly.

'God bless you,' he mumbles in relief. '*Chal phataphat stretcher la, bande bula* [Go, quickly get the stretcher, call the boys],' he tells Parimal, '*Pehle Vikasi ko evacuate karenge* [We shall evacuate the Vikas soldier first]'.

The noise of the rotor blades is deafening now. The first Cheetah appears before them, large and aggressive, hovering above the makeshift helipad that the men have hastily prepared by clearing rocks. The young doctor and four soldiers run towards it with the injured man on a stretcher, their clothes lashed by the draft of the chopper blades. Parimal opens the door of the hovering chopper and they quickly get the wounded inside. Gary steps in holding the saline bottle, thankful that it is connected to a Teflon intracath and not a stainless steel needle that could have torn open his patient's vein during the aggressive running. Tying it to the back of the pilot's seat, he hears his patient moaning and hastily calls out,

'*Hospital ja raha hai, chinta na kar. Ab tu theek ho jayega*
[You are going to the hospital. Don't worry, you will be
fine now].'

Even as the enemy directs another burst of mortar
fire at the chopper, he leaps out and slams the door shut,
sprinting towards the cover of rocks. He and the other
soldiers run with their heads down to dodge not just the
Cheetah's deadly rotating blades but also shrapnel from
the enemy shells bursting overhead. The anonymous
pilot, watching them from his cockpit, raises a thumb in
silent admiration. If he could, Gary would have returned
the compliment but he is too busy running to save his
own life. Lifting off a few feet, the helicopter quickly
drops down into the gorge to avoid getting hit and slowly
disappears.

The second chopper is rising up from the valley now,
as if in slow motion, its big nose emerging at Gary's eye
level, followed by its massive rotating blades. The men
place Jaggi on a stretcher, with Gary again holding the
bottle of saline.

As the chopper swoops down over the helipad, Gary
yells, '*Daudo* [Run]!'

The soldiers run with the stretcher, ignoring the air
bursts, risking their own lives to give their grievously
wounded comrade another chance at his. 'If a bullet does
not have your name written on it, it cannot touch you.'
This is what soldiers often tell themselves during a war
to keep up their courage. And maybe it is actually true

because, on that cold morning in Muntho Dhalo, not one man is touched by the shelling in all six evacuation runs that they do.

Muntho Dhalo

Muntho Dhalo is a flat tabletop feature with a sheer drop into the valley on one side and towering grey mountains on the other. The soldiers of 5 Para wrested it from the enemy only recently and an attack base has been set up. Further attacks are being launched from here. Area Boulders, where the men now live, is so named after the massive boulders scattered around.

For two days, the soldiers survived on the shakkarparas in their backpacks but then an Army Aviation helicopter dropped sacks full of khasta puris. The dirty, starving paratroopers dragged these behind the rocks, slit them open with their bayonets and chewed on them like hungry animals.

That morning, six Cheetah helicopters, flying in pairs to ensure their own safety, swoop down on Area Boulders to pick up the two immobile casualties and the six mobile ones. They also bring life-saving medical supplies that are fast running out in Muntho Dhalo—IV fluids, injectable painkillers and antibiotics—required for the gruesome battle ahead.

Once all the wounded have been evacuated, and the precious new supplies carefully stocked, Gary breathes a sigh of temporary relief. He and his men squeeze into the clefts between the rocks and try to rest.

Amazing Courage

Gary closes his tired eyes but his mind goes back to the terrible casualties they have had so far. He remembers the soldier who was brought to him with his leg blown off. Seeing Gary he had smiled through his pain and said, '*Daktar Sahab, aapke paas pahuch gaya hun, ab sab theek ho jayega* [Doctor Sahab, now that I am with you everything will be fine].' He remembers the paratrooper whose arm had been sliced off by deadly shrapnel, the severed limb carried in by another man. When someone asked about the time, the wounded soldier had replied, '*Meri bazu pe ghadi bandhi hai, usmein dekh lo* [My severed arm has a watch on the wrist, check on that].'

He salutes the courage of the men he is taking care of. He is overwhelmed by the faith they show in his abilities. Though he and his nursing assistants have set up a Regimental Aide Post under a plastic sheet stretched between two boulders, they only have very basic life-saving medicines. Because they are in the enemy's small-arms fire range, the wounded are examined in concealed torchlight. Planks of wood snapped off ammunition crates left behind by enemy soldiers are used as support for fractured limbs, rifles are tied up with line beddings as splints, blood pressure is regulated through IV fluids and compression bandages are applied to stop bleeding from wounds that can cause loss of consciousness and death. The cold freezes him to the bones but Gary is thankful for the fact that it also constricts veins and arteries, reducing blood loss in his patients.

Attending to the grievously wounded without proper medical supplies is not easy. It is akin to working with his hands tied behind his back. But Gary reminds himself, 'I could have been working in a sophisticated air-conditioned hospital outside, but I chose to join the Army. This is what I went to the Armed Forces Medical College (AFMC), Pune, for. This is why I volunteered to be a soldier and a paratrooper, jumping with my men from aircrafts at 1800 feet. This is the job I chose.'

And though there is no one listening to him on those icy, windy heights, he leans back on that barren boulder and makes a fierce promise to himself. 'We are blood brothers, bound to each other by the uniform and the hard-earned maroon beret. I will never let these soldiers down. No man who comes to me alive will be allowed to die.'

It is a promise he does not break. When the war finally ends, 5 Para acknowledges that apart from the soldiers who lost their lives fighting, every injured man brought to the doctor lived to tell the story of that brutal battle.

Siachen to Batalik

Gary's mind goes back to the day when he and the other soldiers had been at the end of their tenure at Siachen

Glacier. It had been a hard year but it was finally over and everyone was looking forward to going back to Agra (where the unit was now posted) and spending two years of peacetime with their families.

That was when the Kargil incursions took place and the paratroopers were asked to report to Batalik. The seasoned, battle-hardy men took it in their stride. They were moved from 102 Brigade to 70 Brigade under Brigade Commander Brig. Devinder Singh, a gunner, paratrooper and aviator, and asked to report at Sanjak, a small village. They travelled there from Siachen base in jeeps and hired trucks, waving to the pink-cheeked, smiling schoolchildren they passed by.

When the soldiers were dropped off at Sanjak, they found that it was a tiny hamlet on the banks of the gushing Indus. There were just about 20 small mud houses scattered around the spot where the Yaldor nullah met the massive river. With all the units of 70 Brigade being launched upward through that axis, Sanjak had been turned into a military camp. While 5 Para's advance party—that included most officers and their CO, Col. A.K. Shrivastava—moved ahead to a place called Ganasok the same night, the main body of 350 soldiers, including JCOs, was left behind. Two young officers—Gary and Capt. Sameer Singh Bisht, another gutsy paratrooper itching for a fight—were given orders to lead the main body to Ganasok the next night.

A Tricky Climb

June 24 1999
7.30 p.m.
Sanjak

The night is dark and cold but the Siachen down-feather jackets are keeping the paratroopers warm. Led by Bisht and Gary, all 350 of them are walking on a precarious track along the deep depression in the mountain, the Ganasok nullah. Their backpacks are heavy with emergency rations, sleeping bags, the Hanuman Chalisa, and the most precious of them all—family pictures wrapped up in woollen vests and dog-eared letters from home that they have read and reread dozens of times. Some of them carry INSAS rifles, others Self-Loading Rifles (SLRs) and AK-47s. Gary and his six nursing assistants carry an additional weight of around 7 kg in IV fluids, injections, a few folded stretchers, bandages, medicines, etc.

The soldiers have savoured the last hot meal they will get for a long time—puris and dal. They carry a few puris and achar in their backpacks and water bottles filled with chlorinated water from the Indus, collected and cleaned at the base camp. They know that after the puris finish they will have to survive on shakkarparas. They are not worried about water because they plan to drink from the fresh water springs scattered all over the area. They later realize how hazardous this becomes. Because of the excessive shelling, all waterbodies are contaminated with gunpowder and the chlorine they carry for water purification does not work on chemical contamination. Nearly all of them are later afflicted with blood dysentery that even the doctor can do nothing about.

Around them, there is pitch darkness, but the peaks above are alive with gunfire. 'We were walking on this narrow, treacherous route along the deep gorge, swallowed by an eerie darkness where one could not see one's own foot, but up on the mountains it seemed as if the sky was on fire. It reminded us of Diwali. There were artillery rounds falling and flashes of light all over. We knew our comrades were battling the enemy and we wanted to be with them as soon as we could,' remembers Gary, talking to me one breezy winter morning, nineteen years later, when the war has almost been forgotten by all except those who fought it.

Unfortunately, the route is so tricky that men frequently stumble and, since they risk falling into the deep gorge on the side, it brings progress down to a slow crawl. Around 8.30 p.m., the two young officers decide that walking in zero visibility is a risk not worth taking. Orders are passed down the narrow file of men. They are told to spread out their sleeping bags and lie down wherever they are in the pitch darkness and get some rest.

One after another the weary paratroopers stretch out on the rocks, groping with their hands to find a place to rest their heads. Some of them drift into disturbed sleep, others just lie back watching the fireworks going on in the heights. They know these are the enemy soldiers raining

mortar fire on the attack teams headed for the heights of
Khalubar, Jubar, Kukarthang, etc. They also know that it
will be their turn soon.

Around 3.30 a.m., when dawn is about to break,
the men get up and start walking again. They reach
Ganasok at 9.30 a.m. where their furious CO has spent
the morning hours pacing around in restless anxiety,
wondering where his men have disappeared. Bisht and
Gary explain to him the risk of trekking up on the
moonless night and are forgiven. The unit 1/11 Gorkha
Rifles (GR) is also in Ganasok and preparing to attack
the ridge of Khalubar that stands before them at a steep
70-degree incline.

5 Para is told to wait for Khalubar to be cleared and
then walk across it to attack Muntho Dhalo. In the next
few days, while the soldiers wait at Ganasok, 1/11 GR
attacks the 5000-metre-high ridge. After a bloody battle
with *khukris* (curved knives used by Gorkha soldiers),
they secure the position even though many, including the
young and fearless Capt. Manoj Pandey, lose their lives.
Manoj is later awarded the Param Vir Chakra.

Now it is the paratroopers' turn to show their mettle.
As night falls, the entire unit, led by Col. Shrivastava, and
a team of 10 Para commandos, crosses the ridge to attack
Muntho Dhalo.

Gary and his team of fourteen paratroopers will not
be part of the frontal battle but they will be the crucial
difference between life and death for many injured

soldiers. It is decided that the medical component will take a different route to Muntho Dhalo so that they reach an easily accessible area called Area Spring and are ready to receive casualties in the direct line of evacuation to Batalik. While the attack companies move forward, Gary and his men walk back for two and a half hours in the dark to reach Yaldor nullah, from where they turn right and keep walking till they reach the last post of 1/11 GR. The Gorkha soldiers advise Gary not to go further because chances are they could be walking into an enemy ambush. Gary ignores their warning and trudges on.

'I knew that the wounded soldiers would start coming any moment and we should reach there as quickly as we could. When a patient is losing blood every second counts,' he explains.

Around midnight, Gary's team faces sudden gunfire. They are being shot at. They jump behind boulders and send desperate messages on their wireless sets to discover that a 1 Bihar patrol has mistaken them for the enemy. Once the patrol is told who they are, the fire is called off and the soldiers start climbing again.

Around daybreak, they see a flat area of land in the distance where Pakistani soldiers are abandoning a post. They are collecting their things, dousing fires, picking up stoves and running with their weapons. Gary is confused for a moment but then he realizes that the Pakistanis are running away from the attacking team of 5 Para descending from the other side.

Since they are completely outnumbered by the enemy, Gary and his team look for cover and hide. They watch the attack and, after 5 Para has taken over the post, they reveal themselves. A delighted Gary calls out to Jaggi, who has led the attack.

Jaggi does not recognize him from the distance. '*Hilna mat, saalon! Goli maar denge. Haath upar karo* [Don't move—we will shoot! Put your hands up],' he shouts.

'Jaggi Sir, it's me, the doctor,' Gary calls out.

'*CO Sahab ka naam bata* [Tell me your CO's name],' Jaggi yells.

'Lt Col. A.K. Shrivastava,' a jittery Gary answers.

'*Unki beti na naam bata* [Tell me his daughter's name],' Jaggi says.

'*Chinki aur Boski* [Chinky and Boski],' an exasperated Gary answers.

Convinced that it is Gary, but wondering if he has been taken prisoner, Jaggi asks the men to walk with their hands up.

When the team is finally recognized, both Jaggi and Col. Shrivastava, who is standing right behind him, are amazed that Gary managed to reach the place even before the attacking body. The young doctor is backslapped for a job well done.

Gary sets up his medical emergency post and gets to work treating the injured. There have been no major casualties since the enemy soldiers lost their nerve and ran away.

'We later found out that the Pakistanis were mortally afraid of both Gorkhas and paratroopers, which—they had found out—were the two units attacking them. Someone had told them that the Gorkhas beheaded people with their khukris and ate them. Paratroopers, of course, have a formidable reputation the world over. The terrified Pakistani soldiers decided it was better to run than fight,' Gary tells me with a wide smile. 'It helps to have a bad reputation sometimes.'

Thereafter, 5 Para sets up camp in Muntho Dhalo and all further attacks are launched from there. The soldiers also manage to clear some area for a makeshift helipad in the pauses between enemy shelling so that choppers can evacuate casualties and bodies of martyrs as well as drop supplies.

Meeting the Daredevil Doctor

When I start writing my book and manage to catch the extremely busy and elusive Col. Vikram Singh Grewal, about whom I have heard so much, it has been nineteen years since the war was fought. He is now posted to his alma mater, AFMC, as faculty. The one-time hands-on war doctor is taking lectures these days; he has his students spellbound with his slide shows on Siachen Glacier and the Kargil War, which I get to see as well.

When we finally sit down to talk, Gary admits that while time has blurred many memories for him, he will never forget the night of 21 June 1999.

'I can see everything happening in front of my eyes as if it were yesterday. The night was dark and moonless. I stood beside my CO, looking at the mountains, trying to assess where our attack companies had reached,' he remembers. 'All we could see were flashes of light up on the barren heights, hear small-arms fire and men screaming in pain. The mood was sombre, the air was riddled with tension and it was frustrating to just watch and do nothing while waiting for the injured to be brought down to us. Around midnight, news came in on the radio set about Jaggi stepping on a landmine. It took the soldiers an hour to get him down to Muntho Dhalo, taking turns at carrying him on their backs.'

Gary says he was relieved to find that Jaggi's entire leg had not been blown up as it was reported but the foot was gone. 'His blood pressure was falling drastically since he had lost so much blood. I knew that our biggest challenge would be to keep him alive through the night and I was desperate that Army Aviation choppers should come and take him to a hospital at first light. The same was true for the Vikasi,' Gary recounts. It all happened according to plan. The helicopters came, the patients were evacuated and their lives saved.

Though he has tended to hundreds of patients and been part of many complicated medical emergencies in the years gone by, Gary says nothing ever gave him more satisfaction than seeing the brave soldiers he treated that night recovering in their hospital beds, when he finally came back after the Kargil War was over.

'They are the reason I can look myself in the mirror and wear my uniform with pride each morning,' he says.

With that, the good-looking doctor picks up his well-deserved maroon beret and, fixing it on his head at a rakish angle, leaves for his next lecture.

A Doctor First, Soldier Later

During his stay in Muntho Dhalo, Capt. Grewal also treated two Pakistani prisoners of war who had been captured alive and brought down by the attacking regiments.

'That day in Muntho Dhalo, there was a lot of antagonism towards the two POWs. Capt. Saurabh Kalia's terrible torture, which we had heard of on the radio, was on our minds and all of us were seething with rage at how he had been treated by the enemy. However, I told the angry soldiers that we could not seek revenge by doing the same to unarmed, injured enemy soldiers who had surrendered. Armies at war have an honourable code of conduct.' That saved the lives of the two wounded and starving POWs who had not eaten for many days.

'The two Pakistani soldiers we were treating at Muntho Dhalo had been abandoned by their own army. Sepoy Hunar Shah of 5 NLI had a festering wound in his leg and could not run with the other soldiers when they were abandoning the post, which is why they left him behind. Sepoy Ahmed Khan of 33 Frontier Force said that he had been sent to Skardu, where he was asked to deposit his uniform and ID card and was sent inside India,' Gary remembers.

'Both the soldiers were tired and petrified of what we would do to them. They were completely broken. Both came from very poor families; they showed me pictures of their children. They also told me that in sheer contrast with how young Indian Army officers led from the front, in the Pakistan Army, orders were always passed from behind. Most of their patrols were led by JCOs and jawans while the officers stayed behind.'

The two POWs were tied up with ropes but they were given proper medical attention, food and water, and then evacuated by helicopter to the base. After the war was over, they were handed over to Pakistan at the Attari border.

'They were our enemies but it was nothing personal. I hope they are back with their families now, living happily. I am a doctor as well as a soldier. But whenever there is a clash between the two roles, I am a doctor first. My job is to save lives,' Gary says

Author's Note

This true story reflects the work that Army Medical Corps doctors and nursing staff did during Operation Vijay. They remain amongst the unsung heroes of the war. Dr Capt. Vikram Singh Grewal and his team attended to seventy-five casualties during the operations conducted around Muntho Dhalo in the Batalik sector. These came from the attacking units in that area—5 Para, 10 Para, 1/11 GR, 2 Vikas and the Engineers. They also treated two Pakistani POWs. All the men who reached Grewal alive lived to tell the stories of their spine-chilling escapades during the Kargil War. He truly honoured the promise he made to himself that cold and bloody night in Muntho Dhalo.

Story 5

Kargil's Only Woman Warrior

In May 1999, twenty-five-year-old tall, slim and soft-spoken Flying Officer Gunjan Saxena, posted at Udhampur with 132 Forward Area Control (FAC) Flight, gets orders to move to Srinagar.

The daughter of an Army officer, Gunjan is looking for action and happy to go to Srinagar. Before leaving she calls up her parents, Lt Col. (retd) A.K. Saxena and Mrs Saxena, who are settled at Lucknow, and tells them that she is being sent out of Udhampur on deployment and might not be able to call them for some time. Being an Army officer himself, Lt Col. Saxena is not unnecessarily perturbed by his daughter's adventures. He wishes her well and puts the phone down.

At that time, the intrusions in Kargil have just started coming to light and no one has any inkling about the

161

magnitude of the operation. When Gunjan moves to Srinagar she too believes India is facing a small incursion by the mujahedeen.

Four helicopters are positioned at Srinagar Air Field during May. Gunjan, who has been flying Cheetahs for a while, is one of the ten pilots based there. Initially, she causes quite a few raised eyebrows at the pilot briefings since she is the only female in a largely male bastion, but the officers soon get used to seeing her around and start treating her with casual bonhomie. Later, when the conflict escalates and the assignments are considered dangerous, she is asked by her detachment commander if she has any problems operating in the area. She says she doesn't and continues to fly, refusing the option to move out of Srinagar and the danger zone.

Around that time, her parents realize that she is flying over the battleground and her life could be at risk, but being a hard-core Army family, they do not interfere with her course of duty. In the initial phase, the small but sturdy Cheetah helicopters that have an established record in high-altitude flying are sent on surveillance sorties. Gunjan is amongst the pilots who fly into the valley covering the Kargil–Tololing–Batalik area, surveying it from the air and reporting any activity they spot. Often they fly over mountainous terrain where Indian and Pakistani soldiers are firing at each other. Around this time, casualties start being reported. The helicopters now start ferrying wounded soldiers from the heights where a gruesome war is raging.

Gunjan too does her share of medical evacuations, often landing close to 13,000 feet on makeshift helipads, hastily cleared by soldiers at war.

Landing on the helipads, she waits for the injured soldiers to be carried into her chopper. Then, signalling a thumbs up to the battle-weary soldiers watching her machine—only a few of whom notice her gender—she quickly pulls the throttle and lifts off, manoeuvring the Cheetah towards Srinagar and safety. The pilots have to be very careful since they cannot risk their helicopters being shot down.

The Cheetah is adept at high altitude flying but it has no defences against the enemy. Pilots routinely carry assault rifles and pistols to face the eventuality of enemy encounter in case of a crash or capture. Since Kargil is under intermittent enemy shelling through the war months, once, when Gunjan is preparing to take off from the Kargil airfield, an enemy missile misses her helicopter and crashes behind it. Undeterred, she takes off and continues with her duties.

The Cheetahs carry out reconnaissance of enemy territory, bringing information about suspected enemy location for the artillery gunners and fighter pilots, besides dropping food, medicines and other supplies for troops battling the enemy in high-altitude terrain, and landing at great personal risk to pick up injured and dead comrades. They are a lifeline for the infantry soldiers who are risking their lives for their country.

Gunjan operates in the area spanning Kargil–Tololing–Batalik. She conducts around ten sorties over a period of twenty days after which the IAF withdraws its small helicopters, launching full-scale offensive support for the fighting troops, and she comes back to Udhampur. She has attained the glory of being the only woman involved in the Kargil War.

An Army Background

Gunjan came from an Army family and always wanted to join the forces. After completing her graduation from Hansraj College, Delhi, she cleared the SSB entrance exam and joined the IAF in 1994.

She has been quoted as saying, 'One of our main roles (in the war) was casualty evacuation. I think it is the ultimate feeling that you can experience as a helicopter pilot. It is a very satisfying feeling when you save a life because that's what you are there for.'

Army Aviation Corp's Role

Besides IAF helicopters, two squadrons of the Army Aviation Corps participated in the Kargil War, clocking a mind-boggling 2500 missions and 2700 flying hours.

The shrill whine of the single-engine Cheetah and the characteristic deep whirring of its rotors brought a sigh of relief to hundreds of soldiers deployed in the war.

The Cheetah mostly operated at heights touching 18,000 feet, which forms its upper flying limit. Not only did the daredevil pilots of the Army Aviation Corps initially lift troops and carry material to points close to where the bloodiest battles were fought, they dropped essential supplies to the fighting troops and evacuated over 900 casualties during the war, carrying injured soldiers to field hospitals and martyrs closer to their grieving families. They did this with fearless disregard to enemy small-arms and artillery fire, landing and taking off from makeshift helipads.

There are innumerable instances of pilots risking their own lives to save those of fellow soldiers. The Army Aviation Corps was awarded two Vir Chakras, one Yudha Seva Medal, three Sena Medals (Gallantry) and one Sena Medal (Distinguished) for its exception role in the Kargil War.

Author's Note

Flight Lt Gunjan's tenure with the IAF ended a few years after the Kargil War because the concept of permanent commission was not valid then. She is now married to a helicopter pilot in the air force.

Chapter 8

The Legacy

A *four-year-old grows up to fulfil his war widow mother's olive-green dream.*

Pachenda Kalan,
Close to Muzaffarnagar,
Uttar Pradesh
2018

In the small village of Pachenda Kalan lives an eighty-five-year-old farmer. Ever since Mahaveer Singh lost his wife two years ago, he has been slipping in and out of dementia. Most of the time, he lies on his stringed cot and stares vacantly out of the window at the wheat fields in the distance. Nobody knows where his mind travels since he slips into a space where the past and the present blur. In those rare moments when he is alert, Mahaveer talks. Voice cracking with grief, he sometimes mentions the young son he lost in the Kargil War. Sometimes he talks about his grandson who has joined the IMA and will be the first officer in their family of soldiers. When he says this, Mahaveer Singh's old eyes light up and a half-smile flickers on his dry lips.

'*Baap ka naam roshan kar diya usne* [He has made his father proud],' he whispers hoarsely. '*Saare gaon ko mithai khilani hai* [I will distribute sweets in the village].'

---

9 June 2018
IMA
Dehradun

The summer sun is up in the sky, its rays reflecting off spit-shined badges and boots. The passing out parade has just ended. Peak caps and laughing gentlemen cadets are being flung in the air, and caught. Whoops of joy, that can possibly be heard all the way to the hills of Mussoorie (just like the training commands of the drill ustad), are breaking the sobriety of the occasion. Perfectly executed push-ups, on sinewy olive green-shirted arms, are setting a rhythm for the celebrations. The beautifully manicured lawns of Somnath Stadium are basking not just in the warmth of June but also the radiant smiles of happy families. Delighted older siblings, awestruck younger ones, ageing grandparents, grey-haired parents—their hearts swollen with pride—constitute the well-dressed crowd. Handsome young officers—slim and ramrod straight, newly commissioned, resplendent in their uniforms, are being hugged and backslapped, hands are being shaken and foreheads kissed with affection.

Of the 457 gentlemen cadets passing out that Saturday morning, there are a few whose fathers are not around to be a part of this special day. Twenty-three-year-old Lt Hitesh Kumar, granted 2 Raj. Rif. as parental claim, is one of them.

The man who would have been the proudest of Hitesh that morning, Lance Naik Bachan Singh, will never see him in uniform. Nineteen years ago, when Hitesh and his twin, Hemant, were just four, this young soldier of Charlie Company, 2 Raj. Rif., was hit by an enemy bullet on the icy cold peak of Tololing.

Neither Hitesh nor Hemant or their mother saw it happen but the scene is vividly etched in their memories from what Subedar Digendra Singh, MVC, who was also in the battle, has narrated to them that it seems as if it happened in front of them. Towards the end of the battle, a bullet ripped through twenty-nine-year-old Bachan's head, making him sink to his knees, his fingers unclasping from around the LMG he had been answering enemy fire with. He gave it to Digendra and his eyes closed slowly as if overcome by deep sleep. He dropped down, his warm blood staining the snow, his thoughts on his young wife and sons he loved so much, who, during his last moments, were hundreds of kilometres away from him. 2 Raj. Rif. suffered very high casualties in the Kargil War. Four officers, two JCOs and seventeen Other Ranks of the battalion made the supreme sacrifice in the highest traditions of the Indian Army in the conflict. Lance Naik Bachan Singh was one of them.

———

That morning in IMA, there is a hint of sadness in Hitesh's smile for the father who is not there, but in his eyes there is quiet satisfaction. It has taken him nineteen years, but he has fulfilled his widowed mother's dream.

'My husband was a soldier but he always told me that he wanted our sons to become class-one officers. The day he died, I decided that I would make sure both of them became Army officers and joined his battalion,' Mrs Kamesh Bala tells me when I meet her in her Veer Awas flat in Delhi a few months later. Dressed in a pastel green salwar kameez, with a dupatta thrown over her shoulders, she is comfortable in her house, smiling and offering me water and a cup of tea.

But that morning in the IMA, she seems a little awkward at being in such a huge gathering of sophisticated strangers. Dressed in a soft-blue sari, the middle-aged Kamesh, her hair greying at the temples, crow's feet etched softly around her bright eyes, stands still in her son's embrace. With her other son too by her side, his brother's ceremonial cap placed proudly on his head, she lets the tears flow over her cheeks. For the family, it is a moment for commemorating Bachan Singh's sacrifice.

Seven Years

Many Hindu wives believe that each time you take your husband's name it decreases one day from his life. Though he is not around any more, Kamesh still doesn't take her late husband's name. 'He and my brother were in the same unit and he would sometimes come over to my brother's house in Delhi,' she tells me, her face lit up by a shy smile. 'I was eighteen then, had completed grade eight and was living with my parents in the village. Once my brother called me to Delhi and I met him there. He was tall and slim, wheatish in complexion. When I saw him for the first time, in a blue shirt and beige-coloured pants, I thought he had such a gentle smile even though he was a soldier. *Mujhe acche lage* [I liked him].'

There was no conversation between the young couple at that meeting, but they both said yes to the proposal. Six months later, they were married. Seven years later, he was dead. Kamesh was just twenty-six when she lost her husband. Since he was an infantry soldier, mostly posted in field areas, she lived in the village with her parents-in-laws nearly all her married life. Kamesh and Bachan lived together for just five months. She says those were the most beautiful months of her life.

A picture, with Kamesh and Bachan sitting on a stone parapet and smiling into the camera, hangs on her sitting-room wall. She picks it up affectionately and shows it to me. 'He was posted in Udaipur. He would take me out every evening. We talked and laughed so much.'

Bachan was posted in Kashmir when the boys were born. He came to Delhi on twenty days' leave, when his wife was admitted to the Army Base Hospital owing to a complicated pregnancy. The twins were positioned upside down and doctors were very apprehensive about whether they would be able to save both the mother and the babies. The babies were finally born via a caesarean section. When her husband came to see her after the delivery, he was so relieved that they both broke down. *Hum dono hi ro pade*, [We both burst into tears],' says Kamesh.

He soon had to go back. After that, Kamesh says, she just saw him when he came home on leave and he would be amazed at how fast the boys were growing up. 'He wanted them to do very well in life and achieve all that he couldn't as a soldier. He had promised to take us along on his next peace tenure, but then the war started and he told me he had to go for that instead.'

During the Kargil War, Kamesh would be glued to the television all the time. She would keep watching the war reports and worry about her husband. '*Mujhe bahut chinta rehti thi* [I used to be worried]. The children were too young to understand anything; their lives went on as usual.'

His Father's Memories

Hitesh says he has very few memories of his father. 'I was four when he died. I know him more from the pictures we have of him and from what my mother has told us,' he says. 'However, there are a few scenes imprinted on my mind.' He says he remembers a birthday when his father was around. 'We used to live with our grandparents in Pachenda village. It must have been our third or fourth birthday. There were no cakes at that time but I remember him sitting in the courtyard of our two-room house on a stringed cot, while my mother was frying gulab jamuns in a big kadai. Later, my brother and I cut a gulab jamun like a cake,' he laughs.

He also remembers holding Hemant's hand and running away from school frequently, soon after his grandmother left them there, arriving home even before her. 'Both my twin and I were quite notorious. We hated school and would frequently run away. I have a very vivid recollection of my father getting really angry about it. I remember him pulling me by one arm, while my grandmother is holding the other one. He is telling my grandmother that he will take us to the city because we were getting completely spoilt in the village,' Hitesh tells me with a smile. 'Eventually, he did shift us to a one-room flat in Muzaffarnagar and got us admitted in lower kindergarten in a Hindi-medium school called Lakshmi Public School.'

Hitesh remembers that when his father came home on leave, he would take the boys to school and sit outside to ensure that the two did not run away. Since they both loved milk, he would also carry bottles of milk for them. After school was over at noon, the three of them would walk back home holding hands, the twins sipping their milk noisily. In the evenings, he would play with them and, after dinner, he would take both of them to the Adarsh Colony crossing to buy them gajak and peanuts.

'We stayed on rent in a single room. Since we did not have a television set, my brother and I would run off to the landlord's house to watch TV, embarrassing our mother. I remember when my father came home on leave, even though he did not have much money, he managed to buy a BPL colour television set for us, so that we would stay home. That TV is still there in our house in Muzaffarnagar; it still runs,' says Hitesh. 'Every time I see it I remember how all of us would sit in the same room—my brother and I would be studying, my mother would be chopping vegetables for the next meal and my father would be watching TV. If we looked up, he would hit us on the back of the head and say "*padhai karo* [study]!"'

This is probably the most endearing memory Hitesh has in which his whole family is together. The other memories are from his father's haunting funeral that he and his brother watched standing in the sugar cane field, not really understanding what was happening.

Kamesh remembers receiving a reassuring letter from her husband from the battlefield. 'I am fine. Don't worry about me,' it said. 'Take care of yourself and the children. The boys have their summer holidays. I think you should go to your parents' house and spend some time with them. *Tumhara man laga rahega* [You'll be happier],' it read.

Soon after, when her husband's uncle came to take her to her in-laws' home, she showed him the letter and said she would prefer to go to her own parents' home. Her in-laws agreed and so she and the boys went to Kutbi, where her parents lived.

Four days later, their small world collapsed.

———

13 June 1999
Kutbi village,
25 km from Muzaffarnagar

Not yet five, Hitesh and Hemant are playing outside the small mud-and-brick house that belongs to their grandfather. The phone has been ringing for a while.

Throwing his plastic bat aside, Hitesh hurries in to answer the phone, almost tripping over the doorstep. Standing on his toes, he picks it up and says, 'Hello?'

His maternal uncle, Rifleman Rishi Pal, is at the other end. '*Beta, apni maa ko bula de* [Son, call your mother],' he says.

Carefully placing the receiver down, Hitesh runs upstairs to find his mother. Kamesh takes the call while he runs out to play. He has just picked up the bat and is telling Hemant to bowl when he hears her sobbing loudly.

The boys stop their game and walk over to the glass window from where they can see their mother. She has tears streaming down her cheeks. Their grandmother too has come downstairs by now. The brothers, who will turn five on 23 October, stand there in the sunlight with their noses pressed against the window, watching their grandparents' house slowly fill up with villagers. The wailing of women rings out around them, making them break into tears as well. They have no idea though why they are crying.

'We were too young then to understand the enormity of the event. Our father had been shot in the head and my uncle, who was also posted in 2 Raj. Rif., had called up to inform my mother,' says Hitesh, talking clinically about the life-shattering event that left him fatherless at four years of age.

Soon Kamesh's in-laws came and took her and the children to Pachenda Kalan. Hitesh says he clearly remembers the day his father's body arrived.

'A huge crowd had collected outside our house. Both my brother and I were also curious to see why. We tried to push in through the sea of people but we were too small to be able to. We even climbed up to the roof of our house but couldn't see anything even from there. Finally, my paternal uncle came and took us down to where the body was kept. It was covered in a white solution and didn't look like the father we knew at all. I don't think we even understood what had happened, but my mother tells me that we cried for a month without having any idea about why we were crying. I remember the cremation. Both my brother and I held hands and went across to the sugar cane and wheat fields where it was being done. Dressed in identical shorts and shirts, we stood at a distance watching his body burn and the red flames licking the sky. Of the few memories I have of my father, that image is the clearest,' he says.

Kamesh says that when she lost her husband, her world was shattered. People who came to console her would always tell her that time would heal all wounds.

'*Kehte the, samay ke saath dukh kam ho jaata hai. Par aisa nahi hota. Dukh kabhi kam nahi hota* [They said time heals all wounds but they were wrong, the sadness never goes away],' she tells me, her eyes moist again.

When Hitesh became an officer that day at IMA, she says she missed her husband the most. She cried for what he had gone without seeing. '*Unhone usse char saal ka dekha tha. Bas ek baar usse afsar ki vardi mein dekh paate toh kitne khush hote* [He had seen his son when he was four. If only he could have seen him wearing an officer's uniform].'

My Mother's Dream

Hitesh says the first time he publicly voiced his desire to join the Army was when he was in grade five in Sanatan Dharm Public School, where he and Hemant were admitted after their father passed away.

'One day, our class teacher, Manju Mittal, who was our favourite, asked the children what they wanted to be when they grew up. When it was my turn, I got up and said, '*Mujhe Army mein jana hai* [I would like to join the Army].' Hitesh says he hadn't thought about becoming an officer till then. 'Both my brother and I were happy to become soldiers, but our mother had bigger dreams.'

Hitesh acknowledges that in spite of her limited exposure and education, his mother was insistent that the brothers should join Rashtriya Military School, Chail, on the advice of Birender Singh, an elder who was also in the Army and whom the boys addressed as Dada (grandfather).

She got them to Delhi to write the entrance test for the school but was disappointed when the boys could not clear it. Birender Singh advised her to send them both to Dehradun to attend coaching classes.

Since they had nowhere to stay, she found a boarding in Garhi Cantonment, where the brothers stayed for six months and attended classes. In their next attempt both of them managed to clear the entrance test.

'It was a tough decision for my mother to let us both go away for our schooling, but she did it for our good,' says Hitesh.

For seven years, while the boys studied from grades six to twelve, Kamesh stayed alone in Muzaffarnagar, hoping her sacrifice would give them a better future.

Lonely Years

Kamesh calls those seven years the most difficult period in her life. 'I just lived for the next time I would see them. I lived so far that I could visit them only once in two months. I also had to run the petrol station back home. They would both start crying every time I was leaving. It was heartbreaking for me. I would tell them to be strong, to study hard.

'"*Beta, Papa ka naam roshan karna hai* [Son, honour your father's name]," I would tell them.' She would then cry all the way back to Muzaffarnagar and, once there, the lonely wait to see them again after two months would begin. '*Bahut mushkil tha per mujhe bahut lagan thi ki ye dono fauj mein jaayein* [It was really tough but I was categorical that they should join the Army].'

Back home, there was very little for Kamesh to do. She would cook and clean and open old albums and look at the pictures facing agonizing loneliness.

'I became depressed. After my husband's death, I lost all confidence. I needed someone to accompany me every time I stepped out of the house. Sometimes my mother-in-law would come and stay with me, but mostly I was on my own,' Kamesh says.

Hitesh says the exposure that he and his brother got in Chail gave them a big boost. 'By the time I was in grade eight, I had come to know about parental claim (where a cadet's wish to join the unit his father served in is given weightage while a regiment is being allocated) and the dream of joining my father's battalion now seemed more within reach. However, since I had only seen soldiers in the family till then, I thought I would become a soldier as well. In Chail, we realized that everyone else wanted to become officers while we were the only two thinking of joining the Army through the ranks,' he laughs.

The twins then considered the option of becoming officers. Though they could not clear the National Defence Academy (NDA) interview, they came to Delhi where they took admission in Shri Ram College of Commerce.

'By that time my mother's dream had become my own,' Hitesh confesses. 'I was crystal clear that I wanted to join my father's regiment as an officer. That was my only ambition. I didn't even consider a second option. If someone asked me what my backup plan was, I had no answer. The truth was that I had none.'

Hitesh appeared for the CDS exam in his third year of college. Not only did he clear that, he also managed to get through the Air Force Common Admission Test and the National Cadet Corps entry scheme.

'I joined the OTA since the CDS merit had not come by then, but after I made it to that merit list as well I took a transfer from OTA to IMA,' he says.

————

The Country Didn't Forget

Hitesh says that the reason his mother could concentrate on her sons was because she had no financial worries. That, he feels, is also why he could focus on his dreams.

'If the country and the organization [Indian Army] had not taken care of us, my mother would have spent her whole life trying to make ends meet,' he says.

The void a soldier's death leaves behind can never be filled up for his family, but what makes his sacrifice worthwhile is the fact that people do not forget him, Hitesh explains. 'It has been nineteen years but people still remember my father. When they see me in the village they still ask, "*Kargil shaheed Bachan Singh ka beta hai na tu* [You are Kargil martyr Bachan Singh's son, right]?" It fills my heart with pride. My father made the ultimate sacrifice for his country. No one can do more than that. The reason my mother and I had no second thoughts about my joining a profession where I might have to go to war too is that my father has been immortalized in public memory. We have no fears. There is a school in our village in his name, Bachan Singh Primary School. The wrestling and volleyball tournaments in the college are named after him. There is a petrol pump, a colony and a memorial dedicated to his memory in Muzaffarnagar.'

Hitesh says the country and the Army took very good care of the families of Kargil martyrs; the country never forgot them. 'They must continue to do that for the families of all martyrs. That will inspire sons to follow in the footsteps of their brave fathers.'

When I get up to leave, Kamesh is sitting beside her other son, Hemant. Hitesh has already joined his father's battalion in a peace station in Rajasthan.

'I feel so proud that Hitesh has also joined 2 Raj. Rif.,' she says, her head held high. When I congratulate her on his success, and hers, she looks me in the eye. There is a steely resolve on her face. '*Abhi toh ye bhi jayega* [He will also do it],' she says, looking with determination at her other son.

Broad-shouldered and handsome, Hemant puts an affectionate arm around his mother. I leave them to their dreams and hope that they all come true.

Author's Note

This story is based on conversations with Lt Hitesh Kumar's twin, Hemant, and their mother, Mrs Kamesh Bala.

Chapter 9

The Man Who Bombed
Tiger Hill

24 June 1999
6.30 am
Adampur Air Base (100 km from the Pakistan Border)

Three Mirage 2000s from 7 Squadron (The Battle Axes) taxi down the runway in complete radio silence. Lifting off smoothly, they make their way towards the India–Pakistan border. Two of them are carrying deadly 600 kg laser-guided bombs, while the third has onboard none less than the Chief of Air Staff, Air Chief Marshal AY Tipnis himself. Thirty-nine-year-old Wing Commander Raghunath Nambiar is piloting the second aircraft with Squadron Leader Manish Yadav as his wingman. The two of them have flown together many times in the past, but never before in war. This is a first. They are headed for Tiger Hill.

Former flight commander of No. 7 Squadron, Nambi has been recalled for the mission. He has been handpicked for his vast experience with the Mirage—over 1900 hours— and also since he happens to be a top-notch experimental test pilot. He has left his wife Luxmi and nine-year-old son Ashwin in Gwalior. They know nothing about the dangerous mission he is on. At this moment, however, Nambi's mind is not on his family. He is going over the complicated sequence of steps involved in the drop of the laser-guided bomb (LGB) he is carrying.

It is more than a month since Capt. Saurabh Kalia and his patrol went missing in mid-May. On 27 May, the Air Force lost two fighter pilots and two aircrafts. Flight Lieutenant Kambampati Nachiketa was taken prisoner after ejection when his Mig-27 was shot down, and later the same day, Squadron Leader Ajay Ahuja, was shot dead by enemy soldiers after he had safely ejected from his plane. He had gone looking for Nachiketa when his Mig-21 was brought down. More recently, a Mi-17 helicopter was shot by enemy shoulder-to-air missiles, killing its crew of four brave air warriors. Nambi's heart is seething with rage. Fear is farthest from his mind. He has been trained to kill in the interest of the nation. The opportunity is finally there and he is raring to do the job.

A half-smile spreads across his lips as he looks at the four-inch by four-inch litening pod screen and finds that it has located Tiger Hill in the rugged grey landscape below where all hills look nearly the same. Changing course, he heads for the target and is rewarded with the sight of nine arctic tents lined up on the south face of Tiger Hill. He swoops down to 28,000 feet, which is the designated height for the attack. A pulse throbs wildly on his forehead. Drawing a deep breath inside his oxygen mask, Nambi fixes his sight on the screen before him. The tents are coming closer. His heart beats faster but his hand stays rock-steady on the controls. Nambi is ready to strike.

6 January 2024
Gurgaon

I find myself ringing the doorbell to the Nambiar residence on a bitterly cold January morning. Having walked through a moist winter fog with a biting wind lashing the folds of my jacket, I am wiping tears out of my eyes when the door opens, and am ushered into one of the most beautiful homes I have visited. My mind is a blur of exquisite oil paintings, rich carpets, fresh flowers and beautiful woodwork. Before me stands the distinguished Air Marshal Raghunath Nambiar, PVSM, AVSM, VM & Bar, former Air Officer Commanding-in-Chief (AOC-in-C), Western Air Command, arm outstretched for a handshake.

I spend two fascinating afternoons listening to the Indian Air Force's most distinguished Mirage pilot talk about Operation Safeed Sagar, which changed the course of the Kargil War. An operation that, many feel, has not been given the credit that was due. The Mirages flew in when a cunning enemy broke India's trust and, crossing the international border surreptitiously, sat firmly ensconced at the top of our highest mountain peaks, directing artillery fire on Indian targets and shooting down soldiers climbing up the treacherous mountains.

Had the Mirages not swooped down from the skies and struck the enemy, the Kargil war would possibly have stretched out much longer, casualty rates would have gone much higher and so many more young soldiers would have lost their lives with their families tragically shattered forever. When I mention this to the Air Marshal, he answers it with characteristic humility. 'The Army did its job well. Credit is definitely due to the infantry that went up to fight knowing how tough it was going to be. So many brave soldiers died. We were fortunate that we could play our part and do what we have been trained for,' he says.

From Air Marshal Nambiar, I hear the incredible story of how, in just about a fortnight, the Indian Air Force fitted its Mirage 2000s with LGBs and how the country's most daring fighter pilots got into their G-suits,* holstered the deadly Makarov 9 mm pistols onto their survival vests, and

---

* A G-suit is a flight suit typically worn by aviators that is designed to rapidly inflate and deflate to counteract the effects of acceleration pressure in a plane, such as blood pooling in the lower part of the body and then rushing to the heads, which can cause pilots to pass out.

climbed into the cockpits of their beloved flying machines to wreak havoc on the enemy.

———————

31 May 1999
9 a.m.
Srinagar Air Field

A stocky AN-32, the workhorse of the Indian Air Force, lands with a loud roar at the runway and taxies to a halt. It is bringing thirteen of the country's top guns—Mirage 2000 pilots—from Adampur to Srinagar. The aircraft door opens and they step out one by one; dressed in blue service overalls and boots, Aviators shading their eyes. The pilots are being taken on a sector recce of the terrain where the Kargil war rages and has already seen a tragic loss of young lives. The Indian Air Force has been asked to step in and the pilots are itching for a chance to level the playing field.

After much deliberation, the Mirage has been identified as the fighter best suited for the mission. The reasons are that it flies much above the range of surface-to-air missiles and has a superior navigation system. Pilots have been pulled out from wherever they are posted—air headquarters, units, command formations, etc. to augment the Adampur-based squadron. Two MI-17 1V helicopters wait at the airfield. Although all thirteen fighter pilots can be accommodated in one chopper, two are being used as a precautionary measure to minimize the risk of losing them all in case of an unfortunate air strike. It has just been forty-eight hours since an MI-17 was shot down by the enemy, killing all four onboard, and the higher-ups do not want to take any unwarranted risks.

Posted as the station flight safety and inspection officer, Air Force Station Gwalior, Nambi is one of the pilots recalled for the mission. Climbing into the chopper, he notices that its pilots are wearing bulletproof patkas, armoured gear, Siachen style overalls and carrying INSAS 5.56 mm rifles, which shows they are deployed in war and are ready for the extremely low temperatures the chopper will fly into. The Mirage pilots, on the other hand, have had no time to draw cold terrain gear, though some are carrying borrowed NATO military jackets. Nambiar himself does not have one. He knows that he won't need it inside the chopper since the temperature is regulated but in the unfortunate circumstance that they have to eject, chances of survival in the minus 20-degree temperature are bleak. He decides not to think about it and looks out of the window instead. The chopper is flying over craggy grey mountain peaks. Just as it approaches Drass, there is enemy fire and the pilots decide to turn around. They land at Matayan, a village located approximately 80 kilometres from Kargil, which is the infantry division field headquarters, and ask the fighter pilots to disembark for a briefing.

The pilots find themselves in a verdant location at about 11,000 feet of elevation. It is lush green with clear blue skies and has a gurgling stream flowing across the land in the backdrop of the majestic mountain peaks. It is teeming with reporters and cameramen on their way to cover the war. The pilots are escorted to an underground shelter made with canvas and camouflage nets, where Maj. Gen. Mohinder Puri, the general officer commanding 8 Mountain Div, waits for them. He gives them an area briefing using a sand model, making it clear that enemy positions have not been identified yet. 'They could be anywhere,' he tells them honestly, explaining that troops have been sent out and enemy locations will be identified only when enemy soldiers open fire.

Air Marshal Nambiar says he clearly remembers that cold morning in Matayan even though twenty-five years have passed. 'Captain Saurabh Kalia and his men had gone missing on 15 May, which is when the incursion was discovered. It was obvious that so far, we had no idea where the Pakistanis were sitting. They were observing silently and directing artillery fire at us. The task before us was to locate and destroy them,' he says. The briefing that morning is interrupted by enemy shelling and everyone has to run for cover which is a terse reminder that the country is at war. The pilots are asked to return to the helicopter. They are immediately surrounded by reporters curious about their presence, but all queries are met with a no-comment response.

Just as the pilots are about to board, they see ambulances speeding in their direction throwing up a cloud of dust.

These were bringing injured soldiers from the Drass side. An accompanying doctor requests the chopper pilots for emergency evacuations to which they immediately agree. Injured soldiers are brought on board. Some of them limp their way up while others have to be carried. Their faces are gaunt and weary, and their eyes dull with pain. Most of them have limbs covered in bloodstained bandages. 'It was a deeply disturbing sight,' remembers Air Marshal Nambiar. 'Besides their injuries, they had also faced the vagaries of nature. The icy wind had burnt their facial skin off, exposing the flesh. They looked like they were in extreme pain and fatigue.'

They find out that the casualties are from 18 Grenadiers, a unit that had been on its way back to peace location after completing a tough Siachen tenure and had submitted glacier clothing when it was told to go back since infiltration had happened. Nambiar's attention is caught by a young soldier sitting next to him in the chopper who does not appear to be more than nineteen years of age. 'He looked fine to me but I noticed that he was only wearing one Jungle boot while the other was tied to his belt by its shoelaces. Over the loud whirring noise of the chopper, I asked him why he had done that. He told me that an enemy shell had exploded near him while he was asleep. It had sent a large shrapnel right through one of his feet which would probably have to be amputated. That was when I noticed his bandaged foot. He was carrying his other boot to show his mother how the injury had happened.' Nambiar says that was a very touching moment for him. 'More than the dead bodies, it was this young boy who affected me the most. It was like coming face to face with tragedy.'

The helicopters alter their route to land at Srinagar Army Hospital where the injured soldiers are offloaded and the Mirage pilots taken back to the airfield from where the AN-32 takes them back to Adampur. 'Our hearts were boiling with rage,' Air Marshal Nambiar remembers. 'We were raring to go and teach Pakistan a lesson. There was absolutely no fear,' he insists. 'I had been twenty years in the Air Force and, let's not mince words, we are trained to use violence against people. We are designed to kill in the country's interests. There was someone inimical to our country sitting on top of us in our land and we were totally frustrated since we didn't know where he was and we didn't have the equipment to get him immediately. We were itching to do something but we didn't know what to do.'

The interview is interrupted by loud meowing from Zoya, the Nambiars' sixteen-year-old cat that they have brought back from an Israel tenure. Clad in a colourful woollen jacket, the plump Zoya saunters out of the bedroom where she had been hibernating and gets busy scratching a dining table leg. The Air Marshal makes a dash for the dining room and, picking the disgruntled Zoya up in his arms, comes back to the sitting room sofa. With the cat sitting contentedly on his lap, he continues his story and tells me how all of them waited impatiently at Adampur for orders to join the war. It was time to settle scores with Pakistan and the fighter pilots couldn't wait to get down to doing it.

Finally, Orders to Bomb

22 June 1999
Adampur Air Base

The day the entire squadron has been waiting so impatiently for has finally come. Nearly three weeks after the helicopter recce, orders have finally been received that Tiger Hill is to be bombed by LGBs. A wave of excitement runs down the ranks and files. There has been a valid reason for the delay. Though the Mirage has air-to-ground weapons, it had essentially been purchased as a counter to Pakistan's F-16s; its main function being to shoot down other aircrafts. In an amazing display of efficiency, trials have been conducted in a short span of fifteen days and litening pods have been integrated with the Mirage, which can now shoot LGBs. Ten litening pods had been bought for the Jaguars too but with its extremely accurate navigation system, the Mirage is much ahead in the integration process. While Tiger Hill looks spectacular from the ground and has caught the attention of the media and the nation, from the air it is just a puny peak compared to the Nun Kun and K2, and not at all easy to locate. The Mirage with its superior navigation system, can easily fly higher than the heights that the enemy is sitting on and accelerate up to 1000 km per hour, a mandatory speed requirement to deliver LGBs.

Once the Mirage had been picked as the weapon of choice, there were only two test pilots in the squadron who were considered eligible for the mission. Squadron Leader Tiwari from ASTE (Aircraft & Systems Testing Establishment), who had been supervising the litening trials on Mirages, and Wing Commander Raghunath Nambiar, who had 1900-plus hours of flying experience with the Mirage, the highest to date. The aircrafts were armed with the LGBs in the centre station, just behind the nose (behind the pilot). The squadron had four two-seater aircrafts and eight single-seaters. Two seaters were picked for the job since two sets of eyes could help locate targets more efficiently. Nambi was paired with Squadron Leader Manish Yadav, while Sqn Ldr Narmadeshwar Tiwari and Flight Commander Sqn Ldr Mohan Rao teamed together. 'We were the only aircraft really capable of doing guided bomb delivery at that high altitude. We were like Tigers. We were the only ones who could do it, and were proud of doing what we did,' Air Marshal Nambiar tells me.

———

24 May 1999
6 a.m.
Adampur Air Base

Nambi and Manish walk across to their Mirage 2000, call sign 101 Bravo, helmets in hand. Weighed down by their pressurised G-suits and with Makarov 9 mm pistols nestled against their chests, they are bristling with energy even though neither has been able to sleep the night before. The two of them have synched watches with Radio Akashvani, shaken hands and wished each other luck in the briefing room. They now walk quietly, each lost in his thoughts.

The 5 a.m. briefing had an esteemed guest—Chief of Air Staff, Air Chief Marshal AY Tipnis, PVSM, AVSM, VM, ADC, who landed in Adampur the previous evening to oversee the mission. The attack brief is that the two Mirages from Adampur will get airborne at 6.30 am in complete radio silence and set course in a north-easterly direction where they will rendezvous with two more Mirages from the Ambala-based Tiger squadron that will be on escort duty. Air Chief Marshal Tipnis will be flown by Wing Commander Sandip Chhabra, Commanding Officer of the squadron, in a third aircraft and will watch the operation from the air. The plan is to hit Tiger Hill first and then proceed 30 kilometres northwest to take pictures of Point 4388 (the next identified target), and then finally return to base.

At 6.30 a.m. sharp, the Mirages take off. Their escorts from Ambala join up with them 300 kilometres short of the target, at a point carefully selected to ensure that it is protected from enemy radar coverage. The pilots barely notice the stunning landscape below. The litening pod spots Tiger Hill from about 50 km away and Nambi, who is piloting the second Mirage, is relieved to find that the sky is clear. A day earlier, they had circled it thrice, each full circle taking eight minutes, hoping for a chance to drop the bomb. But a cloud sat over Tiger Hill persistently, like the hand of god making the attack impossible. On their fourth attempt to circle it, Nambi heard Manish yelling, 'Flare left' indicating a missile attack. He instantly hauled the aircraft upward in a steep left turn and commenced dropping flares so that the heat-guided missile would target those instead of the plane. Manish saw the enemy missile lose steam and fall away and the two of them heaved a sigh of relief and headed back home.

Today, they fly directly at a set of nine Arctic tents perched on the south face of Tiger Hill that touches an altitude of 16,600 feet. The white tents, perfect camouflage in winter snow, are strikingly visible in summer since the snow has melted and now stand out in stark contrast against the mountain's black rock formation. Nambi descends to 28,000 feet, the decided altitude for the attack. He realizes that the wind is not conducive to the release of the LGB. Going up is not an option since the laser is known to switch off automatically at around 30,000 feet. Nambi descends further to 26,000 ft, where crosswinds have dropped and everything is perfect for dropping the bomb.

He is taking an operational risk since his plane is now within shooting range of the enemy's shoulder-fired surface-to-air missiles. Pulsing the laser to designate the target, he looks at the litening pod screen and finds that it has calculated the distance to the target. Accelerating to a ground speed of 1000 km per hour, Nambi keeps redesignating the target as it gets closer. At the release range, he presses the trigger. There is a massive upward jerk as the 13-tonne aircraft sheds the 600 kg bomb and jolts under the impact of losing so much weight. Nambi turns the Mirage left and starts climbing up while Manish takes over control of the litening pod, pointing the laser directly at the target. It is tracking the bomb beautifully. Both Nambi and Manish wait with bated breath as they fly away while the dropped bomb continues to fall. It is supposed to take thirty seconds to hit target but feels like eternity. The seconds pass painfully slow and just when they are almost convinced that the bomb is a dud, the pulsating laser hits the target and explodes on their four-inch by four-inch screen. Flames lick the screen and clouds of dense smoke rise from the destroyed target. The two fighter pilots cannot believe their eyes. They have created history. Nambi breaks the radio silence with a loud 'Bundolo', the war cry from the *Tarzan* comics in the fictional ape language created by author Edgar Rice Burroughs that means 'kill'. It is the prebriefed code for success. The mission is accomplished.

There is no time to celebrate as Nambi has climbed back to 30,000 feet to set course for Point 4388. Scanning and photographing Point 4388 for possible targets, they return fifteen minutes later via Tiger Hill and film it to assess the damage. They are thrilled to find that the target has been blown to smithereens. Pleased with their work, they accelerate to 0.95 Mach, setting fuel on fire as they race back home, and reach Adampur Air Base by 8 a.m. On the way back, they spot red smoke rising from the base of Tiger Hill. After landing, they extricate the videotape from the litening pod and head to the crew room for the debrief. The entire squadron gathers around the television set as the tape is rewound and played back. Besides the devastation the bomb has caused, also visible clearly on film are four enemy soldiers rushing across the screen a few seconds before the bomb gets to them. The video taken on the way back from Point 4388 also reveals a person 2,000 ft below the hilltop climbing painstakingly upward to the camp.

Kreegah! Tarzan Bundolo (Beware! Tarzan kills)

When Nambi and Manish alight from the aircraft, they feel like they are still walking in the air. They have managed to obliterate nine tents on Tiger Hill that were expected to hold a company strength of 15–20 soldiers, besides destroying the arsenal and equipment, and hitting the morale of the enemy hard. It was a huge victory for the country both physically as well as psychologically since Tiger Hill was a roadblock synonymous with the Kargil War.

There are celebratory back thumps and cheers and as the news gets around, and pilots from other squadrons start dropping in to meet the heroes. A Dornier flies in from western command to take the videotape and show it to the higher-ups of the Air Force in Subroto Park, Delhi. The tapes are passed on to Air Headquarters and the political leadership. The super excited air chief calls up Army Chief Gen. Ved Malik from base operations, an underground concealed undergrowth and protected concealed place on an army static switched communication network (ASCON) line. The Army has seen the bombing happening live since units are stationed near Tiger Hill. In fact, that morning they had fired red smoke shells around the base of Tiger Hill to help the Mirages identify the peak. The pilots couldn't see this before the attack since they were flying 30 kilometres away and were guided entirely by the litening pods, but had noticed the red smoke on their way back from the mission and had been grateful for the support.

Air Marshal Nambiar looks back nostalgically at that day. 'I don't claim any special ability other than a lot of experience,' he says. 'An opportunity came my way and I grabbed it. Every individual will get multiple opportunities in life. It is your ability to grasp these that will make you what you are. Tiger Hill was my chance. I happened to be at the right place at the right time. If it was not me, somebody else would have done an equally good job.'

In his guest bedroom, there is a painting of a Mirage flying over land. I miss asking him if that is an artistic representation of him bombing Tiger Hill and whether it is done by Mrs Luxmi Nambiar, who is a gifted artist. But I am assuming it is. I wonder if each time he looks at it, he is reminded of that morning when he made his own contribution to one of the toughest wars that India has fought. Or if he needs a reminder of the day he and his Mirage 2000 created history at all.

At that moment, however, he looks a little pensive since I have asked him how Air Chief Marshal Tipnis responded when he returned from the successful bombing. 'He had known me since I was a cadet at NDA and he was battalion commander,' he says. 'Though there were hundreds of cadets at NDA, he remembered me because I used to be a boxer and was the only one from the third battalion who reached the finals. It was another thing altogether that I got ceremoniously knocked out in the boxing ring in the finals, making him suspect that I had shammed it. He still believes that,' Air Marshal Nambiar tells me regretfully. Twenty-plus years later, the same cadet went on to drop a bomb on Tiger Hill with the chief watching from an aircraft up in the air. 'I hope that made up for the boxing failure and redeemed you in his eyes,' I laugh. 'I hope it did,' says Air Marshal Nambiar smiling widely.

Author's note

After Tiger Hill, six more litening pod-guided bombs were dropped by Mirages during the Kargil War. Air Marshal Raghu Nambiar dropped four of these. Each hit the target perfectly, though he says none was as spectacular as Tiger Hill. By the time he returned to Gwalior, the bombing videos were being shown on television and he had become a hero. Everyone in the Air Force knew him as the man who bombed Tiger Hill and returned home safely.

He agrees that fighter flying is a dangerous business. 'It is possibly the world's most risky profession. The attrition rate is very high. The worry of not coming home is real.' Out of his twenty-eight course-mates, eight had lost their lives by the time he was forty years old. All went in peacetime air crashes. 'It can happen to anyone. But there is so much *josh** in young pilots that all of us fly thinking this will not happen to me.' He too had ejected from his plane (a Kiran aircraft) once when his plane's engine suddenly died.

The Air Marshal, who retired from service four years ago, holds the record for being the country's most experienced Mirage pilot. 'My plane was like a musical instrument in my hands. I knew everything about it,' he remembers affectionately. 'It is four years since I last stepped into a cockpit. But put me there now and I am sure I can do it again,' he says. To me, he sounds endearingly like a twenty-two-year-old pilot officer.

---

* Drive, energy and determination.

Chapter 10

Yeh Dil Mange More

It takes a one-and-a-half-hour flight out of Delhi and then as much time by road to drive from Kangra Airport to Bandla Gaon in Palampur, Himachal Pradesh. The snow-covered Dhauladhar ranges appear and disappear at bends in the winding road, and dazzle you with their magnificence. The fragrant white roses that dot the airport and make the tourists gasp in pleasure follow you all the way to Vikram Batra Bhawan, where the late Captain Vikram Batra's old parents stay in a bright-yellow-walled bungalow. There, they stop and bloom outside the room, where an oil portrait of Capt. Batra hangs on a wall. His father sits before it, draped in a pashmina shawl, asking his wife to get you a hot cup of tea, lay the table for lunch or just corroborate what he is saying from the confines of her bedroom, where she is reading the local newspaper.

On the narrow, meandering path that crosses lush green tea gardens on one side and lazy marketplaces on the other, it is not difficult to get directions to the Param Vir Chakra (PVC) awardee's house. All you have to do is mention his name, and young boys with wispy moustaches, old men with doddering gaits, spectacled tailors with scissors in their hands, and schoolgirls with red-ribboned plaits happily guide you with words and gestures of the hands. You don't really need the address that the gravelly voice of Mr Girdhari Lal Batra, Vikram's father, painstakingly spelled out for you a day ago.

Not very many years ago, a little boy with a puff in his hair and a twinkle in his eye roamed these very walkways, often alongside his identical twin. Luv and Kush. That was what their mother called them. They didn't have a television set at home and would slip their feet into their rubber slippers so they could sneak out of their house to Nisha Didi's next door and watch the TV serial *Param Vir Chakra*, which aired on Sunday mornings at 10. The twins would be shiny-eyed and open-mouthed, marvelling at the bravery of the then-men, who had been awarded Free India's highest gallantry medal. Afterwards, lost in conversation about just how brave the heroes in uniform had been and how awesome the PVC was, they would walk back home.

One of the twins would hold the medal in his hand one day. The other wouldn't, but he would be the one responsible for getting it home—this boy was the feistier of the twins. His name was Luv. The same Luv, whose house a writer would come looking for nearly three decades later. By then, he would have become Capt. Vikram Batra, the twenty-four-year-old soldier who fought for his country in the rocky mountains of Kashmir and died trying to save another soldier.

When she was blessed with twins after the birth of two daughters, Kamal Kanta would wonder sometimes why she had been given two sons when she had asked for just one. 'Now I know. One of them was meant for the country and one for us,' she would later say. All she has of Vikram are the portraits, pictures, medals and memories that she is happy to share.

She remembers the day a colleague at the school where she used to teach told her that she had spotted Vikram at the hospital. Panicking, she had rushed there to find him with a few cuts and bruises on his body, smiling broadly. He had jumped out of the moving bus when the door suddenly opened at a steep turn, and a little girl had lost her balance and fallen off. When his upset mother asked him why he had been so foolhardy, he told her he was worried that the girl would come under another bus.

From his childhood, Vikram was bold, fearless and always ready to help a person in need. Another time, he ran from pillar to post, trying to get a gas cylinder for a new teacher in the school. The teacher had just moved to Palampur and asked for Vikram's help when he had just not been able to manage one despite all his efforts. Vikram promised him that he would get him a cylinder by evening and had kept his word, carting it all the way to the teacher's house in an autorickshaw from the market.

In addition to his gregarious nature, Vikram had a vast circle of friends, an inclination to help anyone and everyone, and a happy temperament. Brilliant at studies, he was also a national-level table tennis player. He was judged the best NCC Air Wing cadet for the North Zone. He had even received a call letter from the merchant navy and got all his uniforms stitched, but at the last moment, decided not to join, telling his beleaguered father that his dream was to become an Army officer.

He took admission in Chandigarh, prepared for the combined defence services exam and got through, just as he had promised his parents. The Batras went for his passing-out parade. Thrilled to see their handsome son in uniform, they wondered just how high he would go. They didn't know then that a few years later, the then Chief of Army Staff, General Ved Prakash Malik, would sit in their house and tell them that if Vikram had not been martyred in Kargil, he would have been sitting in his office one day. It would make Mr Batra's chest fill with pride, despite the tears threatening to spill over.

Yeh dil mange more!

13 Jammu and Kashmir Rifles (JAK Rif.) had completed its Kashmir tenure, and the advance party had reached Shahjahanpur, its new location when it was recalled

because the war had broken out. After crossing the Zoji
La Pass and halting at Ghumri for acclimatization, it was
placed under 56 Brigade and asked to reach Dras to be
the reserve of 56 Brigade for the capture of Tololing. 18
Grenadiers had tried to get Tololing in the initial days of
the conflict but had suffered heavy casualties. Eventually,
2 Rajputana Rifles got Tololing back.

After the capture, the men of 13 JAK Rif. walked
for twelve hours from Dras to reach Tololing, where the
Alpha Company took over Tololing and a portion of the
Hump Complex from 18 Grenadiers. It was at the Hump
Complex that commanding officer (CO) Lieutenant
Colonel Yogesh Joshi sat on the cover of massive rocks
and briefed the two young officers he had tasked with the
capture of Point 5140, the most formidable feature in the
Dras subsector. They could see the peak right in front with
enemy bunkers at the top, but from that distance, they
could not make out the enemy's strength. To Lt Vikram
Batra of Delta Company and Lt Sanjeev Jamwal of Bravo
Company, that didn't matter. They were raring to go.

Col. Joshi had decided that these would be the two
assaulting companies that would climb up under cover of
darkness from different directions and dislodge the enemy.
The two young officers were listening to him quietly as
he spoke. Having briefed both, he asked them what the
success signals of their companies would be once they had
completed their tasks. Jamwal immediately replied that his
success signal would be: 'Oh! Yeah, yeah, yeah!' He said

that when he was in the National Defense Academy, he belonged to the Hunter Squadron, and this used to be their slogan. Lt Col. Joshi then turned to Vikram and asked him what his signal would be. Vikram thought for a while and then said it would be: 'Yeh dil mange more!' (This heart wants more!)

Despite the seriousness of the task at hand, his CO could not suppress a smile and asked him why. Full of confidence and enthusiasm, Vikram replied that he would not want to stop after that one success and would be on the lookout for more bunkers to capture.

Capture of Point 5140

It was a pitch-dark night. Lt Col. Yogesh Joshi was sitting at the base of the hump, from where preparatory bombardment of Point 5140 had commenced. He was trying to make out the movement of his troops, whom he knew would be climbing under the cover of darkness. The Indian artillery had plastered the entire feature with high explosives. For a long time, it appeared as if the mountain was on fire, and Joshi hoped that the enemy on top was dead. His hopes were, however, dashed very quickly. The Pakistanis had occupied reverse slope positions when the Indian artillery was pounding them and had now returned to fire at the Indian soldiers climbing up. From time to time, Joshi would see flashes on the dark mountain. From there, he would know that the enemy was firing at his men and just where the two teams had reached.

The enemy had also started using artillery illumination at regular intervals, which lit up the entire area for about forty seconds. This was done to spot the climbing Indian soldiers. Joshi hoped that his boys were following the standard drill, which was that everyone freezes and tries to blend into the surroundings when the area lights up. Any movement would make them visible.

Suddenly, his radio set came alive, and he could make out the voice of a Pakistani soldier. He was challenging Batra, whose code name, Shershah, the enemy had intercepted. 'Shershah, go back with your men, or else only your bodies will go down.' The radio set crackled, and then he heard Batra reply, his voice pitched high in excitement: 'Wait for an hour, and then we'll see who goes back alive.' At 3.30 a.m., the CO's radio set crackled again. 'Oh! Yeah, yeah, yeah!' Jamwal was signalling that his part of the peak had been captured. Batra and his team were taking longer since they were climbing the steeper incline.

The next hour was to be one of the longest for Lt Col. Joshi. He could hear gunfire and see the flash of gunpowder, but he had no idea what was happening at Point 5140. Finally, at 4.35 a.m., in the cold of the darkness, his radio set beeped again, and he heard the now famous words, 'Yeh dil mange more!' It was Batra. He and his men had captured the peak and unfurled the Tricolour there. What was most amazing was that in this attack, the Indian side did not suffer a single casualty.

After coming down, Batra would call his parents on the satellite phone. For a moment, his father would stop breathing because he would just hear 'captured' and feel that he had been captured. But then the laughing soldier would clarify that he had actually captured an enemy post. He would then call his girlfriend, Dimple, in Chandigarh and tell her not to worry. He was fine, and she should take care of herself. That was the last time he would speak to her.

Vikram's next assignment would be Point 4875, from where he would not come back alive, but he would leave Dimple with memories she was willing to spend a lifetime with. The battalion was de-inducted from Dras to Ghumri to rest and recoup. Less than a week later, they moved to Mushkoh. This was where greater glory was in store for Vikram.

Chandigarh, 2013

Dimple is a pretty, smiling forty-year-old who works with a Punjab State Education Board school in Chandigarh. She teaches social studies and English to the students, checking test papers and planning the next day's lessons. She has no time to even take a phone call. But after she gets back home and sits down with a cup of tea, she confesses that in the past fourteen years, not a day has passed when she has not thought of Vikram.

Chandigarh is full of his memories for her, she says. 'When I pass the bus stop, I remember how I would drop him there so that he could catch a bus to wherever he was going; when I'm in the university, I remember how I first noticed him when he came and sat between me and a guy who was trying to get uncomfortably close, and subtly told me to move from there. When I'm in the Nada Saheb Gurudwara, I remember how he tailed me in a parikrama (circumambulation) and then called out, "Congratulations, Mrs Batra; we have completed the fourth phera (circle), and, according to your Sikh religion, we are now man and wife." 'When I'm near Pinjore Gardens, I remember how before going to Kashmir, he took a blade from his wallet, cut his thumb, and put a streak of blood in my parting to dispel all my insecurities about whether he would marry me or not . . .'

Dimple and Vikram were college sweethearts. They had only attended a few months of classes together at Punjab University when Vikram left to join the Indian Military Academy. They kept in touch and decided to get married. Had Vikram come back from the Kargil War, that was the plan. Only he didn't. Instead, Dimple got a phone call from a friend saying Vikram had suffered a terrible injury and she should call his parents. When she rushed to Palampur, she saw a coffin bearing his body, surrounded by a crowd of media and local people. More than 25,000 had been collected for his funeral, not just from Palampur but also from the nearby towns of Baijnath, Paprola, and Nagrota.

'I didn't go closer because there was too much media there, and I didn't want to break down and create a scene.' She watched quietly from a distance, holding her brother's hand. Vikram's parents noticed the girl in salwar kameez standing in the crowd, but they were too upset to find out who she was.

Dimple returned to Chandigarh and decided she would rather live with his memories than get married to someone else. 'He was a wonderful, fun-loving guy. He was very handsome. He loved to do things for people, but the reason I miss him so much is because he was my best friend. I could tell him my innermost feelings, and he would understand,' she says.

Sometimes, when she accidentally looks at the clock and it shows 7.30 p.m. on a Wednesday or on a Sunday, Dimple's heart misses a beat. For nearly four years, till he went to war from where he didn't return, that was the scheduled time for Vikram to call her without fail, irrespective of where he was. 'He could be in Palampur, Dehradun, Sopore or Delhi, but the call would come, and I would always stay around the phone so that I could pick it up before my father did,' she remembers with a wistful smile.

The telephone no longer rings for her at the allotted time, and even if it does, that familiar voice is no longer there. He would have called, but they don't have telephone connectivity where he is now.

The Last Victory

7 July 1999

The wind was like a knife—cold and sharp—and Capt. Vikram Batra, who had been prompted after his first assault in June, knew it could slice the skin right off his cheekbones. To an extent, it already had.

That was why he and his twenty-five men from Delta Company, 13 JAK Rif., blended in so well with the barren landscape. Their grey, sunburnt faces with unkempt beards and tissue peeling off under the wind's painful whipping, merged perfectly with the massive boulders behind which they were taking cover. Point 4875 was still 70 metres away, and their task had been to reach that ridge, storm the enemy, and occupy the post before daylight. Unfortunately, the evacuation of Capt. Navin, who had a badly injured leg, had taken time, and it was already first light. Through the night, the men had been climbing the slope, with machine gun fire coming almost incessantly from the top of the ridge. Intermittently, their faces would glow in the red light of the Bofors fire that was giving them cover from the base of the Mushkoh valley.

On the morning of 7 July, there was a lot of pressure to proceed. Lt Col. Joshi spoke to Batra at 5.30 a.m. and asked him to reconnoitre the area with Subedar Raghunath Singh. Just before the point was a narrow ledge where the enemy soldiers were, and it was almost impossible to go ahead. There was no way from the left or right either, and, on the spur of the moment, Batra decided that even though it was daylight, he and his boys would storm the post in a direct assault. Setting aside all concerns for personal safety, he assaulted the ledge, catching the enemy unawares, but they soon opened fire. Though injured, Vikram continued his charge with supporting fire from the rest of the patrol and reached the mouth of the ledge, giving the Indian Army a foothold. This was when he realized that one of his men had been shot.

Even as he tried to keep his chin down with a shot whistling over his head, his eyes rested on the young soldier, who had been hit and was lying in a pool of blood just a few feet away. A short while ago, he had been crying out of pain. Now he was silent.

His eyes met those of Sub Raghunath Singh, who was sitting behind a nearby boulder, maintaining an iron grip on his AK-47. '*Aap aur mai usko* evacuate *karenge* [We will evacuate him, you and I],' Batra shouted above the din of the flying bullets.

Raghunath Sahib's experience told him that the chances of the boy being alive were slim, and they shouldn't be risking their own lives trying to get him from under enemy fire.

But Batra was unwilling to leave his man. '*Darte hain*, sahib? [Are you afraid, sir?]' he taunted the JCO.

'*Darta nahin hun*, sahib [I am not afraid, sir],' Raghunath replied and got up.

Just as he was about to step into the open, Batra caught him by the collar: 'You have a family and children to go back to; I'm not even married. *Main sar ki taraf rahunga aur aap paanv uthayenge* [I will take the head and you will take his feet],' he said, pushing the JCO back and taking his place instead. The moment Batra bent to pick up the injured soldier's head, a sniper shot him in the chest.

The man who had survived so many bullets, killed men in hand-to-hand combat and cleared bunkers of Pakistani intruders, fearlessly putting his own life at stake so many times, was destined to die from this freak shot.

When he was in Sopore sometime earlier, Batra had had a miraculous escape when a militant's bullet gazed at his shoulder and hit the man behind him, killing him on the spot. He was surprised then. As he lay dying, destiny surprised him yet again. He had plans to follow, tasks to achieve and an enemy to vanquish. He was surprised that the bullet had found its mark despite all those unfulfilled duties. Batra gasped in disbelief and collapsed next to the young soldier he had wanted to give a dignified death to. The blood drained out of his body even as his stunned men watched in horror.

Spurred by Batra's extreme courage and sacrifice, a squad of ten of his men (each carrying one AK-47 rifle, six magazines, and two No. 36 hand grenades) attacked through the ledge, found the Pakistanis making halwa and killed each of the enemy soldiers on top, with zero casualties of their own in that assault. The fierceness of their attack frightened the Pakistani soldiers so much that many of them ran to the edge and jumped off the cliff, meeting a painful end in the craggy valley.

Even in his death, Vikram Batra had kept the promise he had made to a friend casually over a cup of tea at Neugal Cafe in Palampur on his last visit home. When his friend had cautioned him to be careful in the war, Batra replied, 'Either I will hoist the Tricolour in victory, or I'll come back wrapped in it.'

A tribute by Vishal Batra

If I begin with our journey, it started in a small town, Palampur, in the Dhauladhar ranges in district Kangra.

Luv, as we called Capt. Vikram Batra, PVC (posthumous), and I, Kush, his identical twin (just fourteen minutes younger), had a life full of laughter and pranks till we grew up and decided that we wanted to be part of the Indian armed forces.

How fast time flies! And how all of us don't get what we want. Luv made it into the Indian Military Academy in March 1996, and I, rejected three times by the Service Selection Board, had to settle for a career in management.

When Vikram visited us during his annual leave, looking tall and handsome in his uniform, I realized how much passion I still had for the forces. With great pride in my eyes, I watched my brother march ahead in life so much faster than we had thought.

Having gotten commissioned into 13 JAK Rifles with his first posting in Sopore, Vikram already had some daring face-to-face combat with the enemy in insurgency operations. We knew he was born to fight against the odds.

It was around the same time that the Kargil War happened, and he was asked to move there to help fellow soldiers flush out Pakistani intruders who had entered Indian terrain. The last call Vikram made to Mom and Dad on his movement had given us some jitters, but we always knew that he was a daring officer for whom facing any challenge was a cakewalk. His last statement to one of our friends before proceeding to Kargil, that either he would hoist the Tricolour or come back wrapped in it, still echoes in our hearts. It showed what iron he was made of.

It's been fifteen years. A lot has changed, and a lot has remained the same. I have many more grey strands in my hair. Vikram remains as youthful as ever. Time cannot touch him. In these fifteen years, there has hardly been a day when Vikram has not been spoken about.

The greatest memory etched in my heart so deeply is from way back in 1985, when the Doordarshan-telecast serial Param Vir Chakra. We didn't have a TV then and would watch at our neighbour's house. I could never have imagined, even in my wildest dreams, that the stories we saw in this popular serial would one day become so real for us. Or that Vikram would be the hero. The famous radio message, from a height of 18,000 feet, 'Yeh Dil Mange

More', by Vikram caught the fancy of millions of Indians, and they still haven't forgotten it. Or him.

So many times, strangers come up to me and tell me that I look like Vikram or ask if they have seen me somewhere. I have been asked by hundreds of people if I am related to Vikram. Each time, I know they are thinking of Vikram, and I feel proud to be his brother.

Death is the ultimate truth of life, but how many of us have the courage to face death with open arms? My brother Vikram was a Param Vir—Bravest of the Brave.

I salute all those soldiers who are the real Virs (heroes) of this nation.

Chapter 11

The Fearless

Batalik sector, Kargil
2–3 July 1999

Manoj Pandey sat crouched in a trench, almost blending in with the rugged brown slope. He was watching a burst of Bofors fire light up the purple sky. The unruly stubble on his chin made his face itch. He could smell nausea in his hair even from under his helmet, with a rip in the lining where the hard metal pressed against his scalp—cold yet strangely reassuring. Under the grime smearing his face, his features were good—a well-defined straight nose, a firm mouth and a broad forehead creased in concentration. He did not sport a moustache. His chin was determined, and his eyes were warm, brown, and finely lashed, though at that moment they were bloodshot from a serious lack of sleep. He sat motionless, staring stonily ahead, his rough, weather-beaten hands clasped firmly around his Insas rifle.

A *khukri* (a traditional Nepali dagger) hung from his belt and rubbed against his thigh, the evil glint of its cunning blade sheathed in soft velvet. At the regimental centre in Lucknow, where he was trained to be a Gorkha Rifles soldier, he had been told that it was the best weapon to use in close combat, small and deadly, instilling instant terror in the enemy. He had been trained to slice a man's neck off, cutting swiftly across the skin—right to left, left to right—ripping through veins and sinewy muscles in one powerful move. At the regiment's Dusshera celebration, when he had just joined his unit two years ago, he had been asked to prove his mettle by cutting off the head of the sacrificial goat after the puja. For a moment, his mind had wavered, but then his arms had lifted in the air, bringing the glittering blade of the sharp dagger down on the scared, bleating animal's neck, severing it from its twitching body in one massive blow that sprayed his nervous, perspiring face with warm blood. Later, in his room, he had trembled at the act and washed his hands half a dozen times to take away the guilt of his first deliberate kill. He had always been a vegetarian and a teetotaller.

In the past two months, Manoj has come a long way from his natural humane reluctance to take lives. He has contrived attacks, planned kills and used stealth to surprise enemy soldiers as they sat on craggy peaks. He has climbed freezing mountains, trudging through snow and sleet, without even winter clothing in the initial days. He had used woollen socks as gloves to shield his freezing fingers, peeling them off when they got soaked in a sudden shower, twisting them to squeeze the water out, and slipping them on again. He had fixed targets within the sight of his rifle, taken aim, and pressed the trigger, tracing the bullet's path with his eyes as it zipped through the distance and embedded itself in human flesh. He had killed in cold blood, shooting men through their heads and their hearts, dispassionately watching them bleed to death.

His expertise with the khukri as a weapon of execution had, however, not been tested yet. His instinct told him that tonight could be the night.

Manoj Pandey shifted his weight and winced. The edges of his briefs were cutting into his groin. Every time he moved, the rough fabric would slice through the raw skin, digging a micro-inch deeper. He had been wearing the same clothes for almost a week.

Running a hand across his soiled combats, he felt the murky stiffness of sweat and grime. His fingers hovered over the rips and tears where the fabric had been ripped threadbare by crawling on razor-sharp rocks. But there was consolation in the company. Cocking his head slightly, he silently observed the dark outlines of his men—short, stocky Gorkhas—grouped unevenly around him in the darkness—dirty, starving, and battle-fatigued, yet brave.

He made no sign, his eyes remained dark and languid, and no emotion flitted across his face. But for them, he felt deep warmth in his heart.

The sun had disappeared, dropping an impregnable black quilt over the terrain. It had the crisp green of the grass, the blue rush of the sparkling water, and the mesmerizing beauty of the district, and he preferred it that way. Daylight just added to his outrage at Pakistan's audacity to sneak in and occupy the heights around them. Emotion interfered with resolve; tonight, all he needed was cold reason and an animal's instinct for survival.

Somewhere behind him, in the gloomy darkness intercepted only by the calls of crickets, the Ganasak Nala gurgled, lapping against the quiet of the still night. Ahead loomed a steep, though blurred, 70-degree incline. That was Khalubar, the 5000-metre-high ridge he and his men had to climb that night. Their task was to reach up undetected, take the enemy by surprise and destroy the Pakistani bunkers on top before daybreak.

He knew not many of them were expected to return, but that didn't bother him much. He remembered the emotional words he had once scrawled in the depths of a diary he had been maintaining since childhood: Some goals are so worthy; it's glorious even to fail. Signalling to his men to follow with a curt nod, Manoj got up, slung his gun behind him and started to walk.

They had been on almost continuous assignments for over a month, one following the other. In the army, they called it a rodent's life—scampering up hillsides under cover of darkness, finding holes to crawl into when daylight broke, while carrying their backs 4-kg backpacks that held sleeping bags, extra pairs of socks, shaving kits, and letters from home. They would nibble on hard, stale puris when hunger struck. Though the nala was close with its freshwater beckoning, they could never reach it because the enemy would fire from the top. Instead, they would reach into crevices to snap off icicles that they would suck greedily on to quench their thirst. They would fill their water bottles with crushed snow for the endless rocky climbs, where water would not be found and crack icicles under their teeth, swirling them around in their mouths like the coloured iced lollies from their childhood. When Manoj returned to his trench after a taxing assignment, bone-tired and shivering, and closed his eyes for a few moments of respite, images that were hidden in some corner of his mind, carefully wrapped in the cobwebs of time, came back to haunt him.

'*Bhaiya kuch toh le lo* [Brother, take something, at least],' the three-year-old could hear his mother's voice from somewhere in the distance. His eyes were lost in the cacophony of sound and colour that play an important part in the wooing ritual of young innocents by the habitual seducers in big cities.

It was his first visit to Lucknow, and the little boy from Rudha village, dressed in his best khaki shorts and cotton shirt, was looking with wide-eyed wonder at the new world unfolding before him. He had never beheld these sights before. Around him there were hawkers selling sticks of fluffy, pink candyfloss and bright orange bars of ice cream; crisp golgappas were disappearing into open mouths, and on a wooden cart, a man was grating ice to a fine powder that he would collect in a mud bowl, sprinkle with some bright red syrup, stick a wooden spoon into, and hand over to outstretched arms.

He felt his mother pull on his little hand and suddenly, his senses were assaulted by a big man with a ferocious black upturned moustache and yellow paan-stained teeth that flashed in his face when he parted his lips in a big smile. Behind him, on a wooden pole, were tied balloons and bright plastic toys—pistols with brown butts, squeaky green parrots with shiny red beaks, catapults, whistles and dolls.

What caught his eye was a brown wooden flute, dotted with darker stains. 'I want that,' he told his mother. She tried to tempt him to buy a toy since she felt he would not be able to play with it, but he was undeterred. Finally, she gave up and paid Rs 2 to the vendor. She placed the flute in her son's little hand, quite sure that he would throw it away before the day ended.

She was wrong. The flute stayed with Manoj for the next twenty-one years. He would take it out every day, play a tune on it and place it back in his cupboard next to his neatly folded clothes.

Even when he went away, first to Sainik School, then to NDA, and finally to the snow-clad peaks of Kargil, the flute would remain in his trunk of old clothes and memories that his mother would eventually stop looking at because it always made her cry.

Deep in his stomach, Manoj could feel a faint rumble. He wondered if the man beside him could hear it too. The hunger pangs were striking. There was a cold puri lying in his backpack somewhere, but he didn't care much for it. It was like chewing on cardboard. This time, it was his tongue that tempted his mind to go back to the mess where dosa, sambhar and that spicy chutney called gunpowder would be served on Sunday afternoons for brunch. 'Gunpowder,' he said aloud and laughed dryly. His mind went back to that first Sunday in the regiment when the commanding officer (CO) had asked him for a glass of wine. A teetotaller and new to the Army then, he didn't know how wine was served, and summoning the mess, the waiter had naively asked: 'How will you have it, sir? With soda or water?' The bar had rung out with amused laughter.

Manoj shook his head to shake the memories out of it and concentrated on the task ahead. He and his men had been climbing in miserable darkness for almost nine hours. Most of them had rolled up their jackets and shoved them into their backpacks. Manoj had a pair of spare woollen socks that he had wrapped around the breechblock of his rifle to keep it warm, lubricated and protected against jamming in the cold. A seized weapon in war could make the difference between life and death. On the last mission, a man's breechblock had jammed and he had to hastily light a precious fuel tablet under it to get it back in working order. He didn't want that to happen tonight.

Though the night temperature was touching sub-zero, the arduous climb made the soldiers sweat. Manoj led his men quickly and noiselessly. He would slip his fingers into cracks in the rocks and pull himself up, fleeing his way ahead, deliberately keeping his mind off the fact that there could be a snake or a scorpion sitting in a crevice, ready to strike. The ascent was slow and nerve-wracking. Besides the terrain and the bad weather, there was the constant trepidation that the very next fold in the ridge could be an enemy hideout or a bunker. Every still shadow in a crevice appeared to be a Pathan lurking with a gun. The fear was constant, dogging them at every step, constricting their throats with its suffocating grip, and making goosebumps erupt on their cold, wet skin.

Climbing was a thirst-inducing business and most of the men had finished their one-litre water bottles. They found some patches of snow under larger stones. While some of it was fresh and could be picked up in greedy fistfuls to quench thirst, most of it was too contaminated by gunpowder to be of any use. Manoj ran his tongue over chapped lips and didn't reach for water even though he was tempted. There was just one last sip left. He wanted it there for psychological support till the end.

His thoughts went to his mother and lingered lovingly over there. He saw her, brow-lined with worry, gentle and caring in her faded green cotton sari, leaning forward to kiss his forehead softly as he told her stories of Siachen from where he had returned. He blinked the moisture out of his eyes.

As often happens with children who have grown up in humble circumstances, Manoj has always been a careful spender. His father ran a small hosiery business and had a family of three sons and one daughter to bring up. Being the eldest son, his parents' efforts to make ends meet were never hidden from the quiet child, who spoke little but observed a lot from underneath dark eyelashes that were always bent over a coursebook. Manoj had been an outstanding student right from the beginning. He knew he had to do well in life so that he could give his family all the happiness in the future that they couldn't afford right now. He wouldn't ask for new clothes till the old ones started showing tears that could not be darned anymore; whatever he had would be neatly folded and put back in the cupboard. His books, with brown covers, would be put back into his school bag after every use. His notebooks would be filled with neat and steady handwriting, with its delicate right slant, just the way his Montessori school teacher had told him to write; his copies would never have an ink stain or untidy scribbles running across the page. Manoj knew money was short and also the value of each hard-earned rupee. He understood just how difficult it was to get a family two square meals a day and how tough it was to keep hunger at bay.

The train had slowly started moving out of Jhansi railway station. Suddenly, a dark, ugly, wrinkled face thrust itself at him from behind the iron rails of the window. A pair of dull eyes, hazy with cataracts, looked greedily at the shiny, silver-foiled paper plate of food he was holding. A dirty hand shot forth and gestured towards a hollow stomach, with dark folds of scaly skin hanging over the edges of a faded petticoat. '*Bhook lagi hai beta* [I am hungry, son],' the withered old woman grovelled, her grey hair falling untidily over her face.

Before his father could reach into his wallet for some change, Manoj had put his hand out between the bars and handed her the steaming hot plate of chole bhature. The train picked up speed and chugged out of the platform; the old lady was left behind, holding a full meal in her calloused, old hands.

Since he hadn't been well, Manoj hadn't eaten for a day after his passing-out parade at NDA, and his father got down at Jhansi to get him something to eat. When his mother scolded him for giving the food away, he told her affectionately that he was a strong young man and could stay hungry for two days, but the old woman needed to eat.

The men had been climbing for more than fourteen hours. They hadn't slept for twenty-four hours. Sudden downpours of sleet and snow had left them chilled to the bone. They had miscalculated the treacherous path and lost their way twice in the dark, and it was already morning by the time they spotted the hazy outline of the top.

They had the option to go back before the enemy spotted them, but Manoj made up his mind—they would complete the task they had been sent for. There would be no turning back now. They would storm the enemy bunkers, making the best of the bad weather and the wet mist creeping up the cliffs, with its cold fingers on all it found in its path.

Another volley of fire lit up the sky. Manoj knew the guns were lined up on the highway, all along the Indus, firing at least 20,000 rounds at a time. The aim was to distract the enemy, which was why he and his men had been able to climb the 70-degree incline unnoticed so far. However, this time the fire seemed to be dangerously close. The burst of shells was accompanied by a hail of bullets, and suddenly a soldier screamed out in pain and collapsed.

'Take cover,' Manoj shouted, 'this looks like enemy fire'. The bullets, rockets and machine gun fire were coming at them with an unnerving accuracy. The cries of men who had been hit rang out through the stillness of the chilly morning.

From behind the boulder where he had taken cover, Manoj looked out. Around him was death and destruction. Limbs had been torn apart, flesh ripped into, and blood was seeping into the soil as the gut-wrenching screams of his men echoed in the impersonal stillness of the bare brown mountains.

He knew they would have to storm the enemy in a daring daylight attack right now. As soon as his mind was made up, the rush of adrenaline overcame indecision, fear and nervousness. The paralysing cold seeping into his bones was replaced by the heat of blood coursing through his veins. As the tracer bullet came flying past, lightning the place with a deadly cocktail of shrapnel and fire, Manoj stood up, tall and brave, his slight frame coiled like a spring, his face a mask. Through the scream of the wind, he roared at those of his men who were fit to fight, ordering them to follow him through the hail of bullets. Like a colossal god with invincible powers, he walked into the curtain of shells and bullets. He didn't look back even once to see who had followed his final command, but if he had, he would have been a satisfied man. All his Gorkha jawans, who could pick themselves up and walk, were right behind him, their khukris gripped firmly in their hands.

Leaving behind those dead or dying, the men charged like angry lions, placing their feet firmly on the sleet-covered jagged rocks, following the man who was not walking through flying bullets for the first time. They had seen him do it before. Just about a month ago.

About a month ago

In a narrow gulley, the bodies of four men from an ambushed patrol had been lying for more than ten days since the Kargil War had started. They were from an initial patrol that had been sent to reconnoitre the occupied heights when the Indian Army had grossly underestimated the enemy Infiltration. Completely unaware that they were being watched by the Pakistanis from both sides of the gulley, the men had walked into a deadly trap. They were shot dead at point-blank range by enemy soldiers sitting at a height on both sides. All efforts to retrieve the bodies were repulsed by the Pakistanis, who would start firing indiscriminately the moment they spotted any activity from the Indian side.

Manoj volunteered to go and get the dead men back, insisting that their bodies be wrapped in the Tricolour and sent home to their families. He and his men had crept behind boulders and climbed the heights, reaching higher than the enemy. Then, while some men were engaged in firing, the officer and a few of his men crawled down to where the bodies were lying and, ignoring the hail of bullets flying past, dragged the bullet-riddled bodies out of the gulley.

Manoj had been one of the first to reach and had boldly crawled up to a dead man, pulling him behind a boulder. For a moment, he stopped to look at his dead mate and his heart burned with rage. The body was badly mangled by shrapnel and he couldn't make out the man's face. On his bloody finger, there was a gold ring that told him the man had probably been married. Even the belt he wore around his waist was punctured with bullet holes.

'You bloody dogs, I'll throw you out of my country,' he had promised the enemy, shouting out in anger, and had then used all his strength to drag the dead soldier back.

It was a miraculous retrieval, and even a decade later, officers who had watched the operation would sit with a glass of whisky in the mess and remember the amazing man who had managed the impossible. 'It needed a very big heart to do what he did,' they would say. 'Only he could have done it.'

The time has come to show that daring once again and Manoj does not disappoint his men. Adrenaline coursing through his veins, he gestures to them to follow and, steeling his heart against every instinct for self-preservation, walks into the curtain of flying bullets to reach the first bunker on the ridge—a pile of cut rocks with a boulder for a roof, grainy in the brooding fog that is sweeping across the landscape. He can make out the shadowy outlines of two Pakistani northern light infantry soldiers. He is not conscious of an effort, but a sharp tug at his belt apprises him that his hand has gripped the handle of the khukri hanging there and whipped it out in a silken move. The sheath falls away limply by his side as his hand flashes its ferocious blade up in the chilly wind. The thumping of his heart is left behind in an instant as he runs across the uneven terrain, jumping over boulders in the falling snow, his face a grotesque mask of death, and falls upon the enemy soldiers, ferocious and proud. There is a swish in the air as the blade cuts through the falling snowflakes, flashes, and slices into human flesh.

Right to left, left to right. Then again. And again. The bodies of the shocked Pakistanis, terror written in their eyes, fall in a bloody pile. They could have never imagined that someone would walk in through the deadly fire. Had he been watching, the young officer's regimental centre, khukri ustad would have been proud of his student as he let the blood drip off his khukri and looked up to find his next target.

Sprinting across to the second bunker, the men fiercely pounce upon the enemy, and bloody hand-to-hand combat follows, '*Jai Mahakali, Ayo Gorkhali*' piercing the cold morning. Return shots ring out. Some of the enemy soldiers are charging with their bayonets, but most find they are no match for the gusty Gorkhas with their lethal khukris that are splashing blood on the wet rocks. Suddenly, Manoj winces. He has been hit in the shoulder by a bullet. Unconcerned and feeling no pain in the heat of the moment, he takes out his gun and moves on to the next bunker, spraying the ones hiding there with a shower of bullets.

Another bullet comes and hits him in the leg, making him stagger unsteadily. '*Naa chodnu* [Don't leave them],' he cries out in Gorkhali, telling his men to carry on the carnage, and drags his injured leg forward. Reaching out for a grenade, he lobs it at the fourth bunker, from where mortar fire is coming at them. Even as an explosion rents the sky, throwing up a dull grey cloud of stone and debris, a fatal shot bursts through the air and hits the officer in the forehead. There is a flash of yellow, and he is engulfed by the smell of burning cordite and warmth in the freezing cold. His whole body is wracked by terrible pain—his brain is on fire, his lungs are gasping for breath, his heart seems to want to force itself out of his chest, and his tongue is dry and swollen with thirst. He wants to go on and shoot the Pakistani soldier he can see leaping out of the burning bunker and racing down the slope, but his disobedient body has stopped listening to his commands. He can only watch as his arms let go of the rifle he has been holding, his fingers lose their grip on the trigger, his knees buckle under him, and his neck slumps forward on his heaving chest. Blood courses down his face, blurring his vision. There is a spurt of light in his head, then stark darkness and silence. Finally, he has to close his eyes.

Manoj Kumar Pandey of 1/11 Gorkha Rifles is dead—his blood-stained body tilts in an arch and falls gently to the ground in the fourth bunker of Khalubar. He is twenty-four years and seven days old.

About six years ago . . .

On a warm, sultry summer afternoon, a thin boy with a side parting in his hair and shiny new leather shoes walked down for his service selection board interview for NDA. He was trying to keep his mind off the bite in his toes, the string of cheap elastic in his socks, and the guilt he had felt asking his poor father for money to buy them. He reminded himself that he was the best NCC cadet in his state and desperately hoped that his basic knowledge of English would not desert him during the interview.

'Why do you want to join the Army?' The interviewing officer was stern and abrupt, looking straight into his eyes.

'I want to win the Param Vir Chakra,' he replied, returning the stare, hoping the sentence was grammatically correct. The interviewing officer looked at the others on the board and exchanged a smile.

Sometimes, they say, there is magic in the air, and we must be careful about what we say because it will come true. Not only did young Manoj Kumar Pandey from Sitapur district in Uttar Pradesh get into the NDA, he also won the Param Vir Chakra, the Armed Forces' highest gallantry award. Unfortunately, he hadn't said he wanted to wear it alive.

People and Organizations
Working for Martyrs

This is a list of some people and organizations that work for the cause of the martyrs and their families. Please feel free to look them up and/or join them if you desire.

Honourpoint: It is an online memorial to honour and remember martyrs. With nearly every martyr listed on its website, Honourpoint is an effort to ensure that the sacrifices of soldiers and their families remain in the nation's collective consciousness. For more, visit: www.honourpoint.in

Vasantharatna Foundation for Arts: It is run by Mrs Subhashini Vasanth, wife of late Col Vasanth V., Ashok Chakra, who was killed in action while trying to prevent heavily armed infiltrators from crossing the India-Pakistan border at Uri in 2007. The foundation attempts to keep the memories of martyrs alive by instituting memorial awards in their name at educational institutes and asking their widows to give these away. Mrs Subhashini received the Neerja Bhanot Award for her exemplary services towards the families of martyrs.

Martyr Captain Tushar Mahajan Memorial Trust: It was started by renowned Udhampur educationalist and retired principal Dev Raj Gupta and Asha Rani Gupta, in the memory of their son—Capt. Tushar Mahajan, Shaurya Chakra, 9 Para (SF)— who lost his life during a militant attack in Pampore, J&K, in 2016.

Jitendra Singh: A security guard from Surat, Gujarat, was unable to make it to the Army but decided to do whatever he could for the men in uniform. He has written more than 4500 letters to the families of martyrs and tries to visit them too. He dreams of opening a museum in Mumbai.

Rashtriya Riders: Himmat Singh Mandrella heads this group of riders who ride to the places where soldiers fought. They also visit the families of martyrs. For more, you can visit their Facebook page.

Heroes in Uniform: It is run by Sonali Singh, the daughter of a soldier, who spreads stories of the courage and sacrifice of our soldiers so that they are not forgotten. She also runs initiatives to equip retired soldiers with skills that allow them to take up new jobs (having trained close to 450 so far), runs entrepreneurship programmes for soldiers' families and organizes fundraisers for those in need. For more, you can visit the Facebook page.

Major Akshay Girish Trust: Set up by the family of this young officer who led an attack against heavily armed terrorists and fell fighting after being hit by multiple bullets in Nagrota in 2016, the trust promotes nationalism, and motivates and helps those striving for a career in the armed forces. For more, visit: https://majorakshaytrust.org/.

Portraits of Patriots: Delhi-based art teacher Hutansh Verma pays tribute to the brave soldiers by making portraits of them and personally delivering them to the families. He does not like doing this in public functions.

Martyr Tushar Mahajan Trust: The trust presents awards and scholarships to meritorious students, besides conducting medical camps and a host of other social programmes. Capt. Tushar Mahajan of 9 Para SF was killed in action while leading a daring midnight operation to rescue hostages in the Pampore attack in 2016. For more, visit: www.facebook.com/captainTusharMahajan9Para/.

Maj Mohit Sharma Foundation: Maj. Mohit Sharma, Ashok Chakra, SM, of 1 Para SF, laid down his life battling terrorists in the Hafruda forests of J&K in March 2009.

His family runs this foundation in his name and organizes a number of social programmes and initiatives for those in need. For more, visit: www.majormohitsharma.org and www.majormohitsharmafoundation.blogspot.com.

Acknowledgements

I am grateful to the families of our martyrs for sharing with me their memories of the men they loved and lost. I hope my stories do justice to these precious remembrances.

I am thankful to the brave soldiers and officers who fought the Kargil War and took out time to share their experiences with me. Without them, this book would not have been possible. I would also like to thank the Additional Directorate General of Public Information (ADG PI): Col. A.R. Singh, director, ADG PI, for being a pillar of support at all times; Col. Saji Abraham, for being my guide and facilitator; and Maj. Dibya Satapathy, for sifting so painstakingly through war pictures to help find photographs for this book.

It was a pleasure working with Gurveen Chadha, my book editor: sincere, meticulous and as passionate about making *Kargil* the best book we could as I was. She shared my respect and concerns for the men in uniform. I am also grateful to Gunjan Ahlawat, head of design at Penguin Random House India, for creating a cover that captures the spirit of the war.

And, lastly, I would like to thank my husband, Col. Manoj Rawat, for reading initial drafts, for dropping and picking me up from airports and train stations, and for ruling with an iron hand our two boys, Hukum (the crazy golden retriever) and Saransh (the wise teenager), single-handedly while I was away or writing obsessively.

A thank you is also due to my kid brother, Col. Sameer Singh Bisht, SM, VSM, for sharing his Kargil War experience with me, for finding stories and phone numbers for me, and for being my sounding board at all times. He stepped in to be the first reader of the complete manuscript since Dad was no longer around to do it. 'It's come out very well. Good job!' he said as I waited impatiently for his verdict. It's strange how I sometimes see my dad in him.

The people we have loved and lost might never come back, but they continue to live in the ones left behind. That's what researching for *Kargil* has taught me. And that's what writing it has taught me as well. I am grateful for it all.

Scan QR code to access the
Penguin Random House India website

Vikram Batra being pipped by his proud parents at the Indian Military Academy passing out parade.

Vikram the soldier.

He was the bravest of our braves: Capt. Manoj Pandey.

The pipping ceremony. At his NDA SSB interview, Manoj Pandey had said that he wanted to join the Indian Army because he wanted to win the Param Vir Chakra. He kept his word.

He went away young, but Manoj proved to the world that he was the epitome of courage and determination on multiple occasions.

Battle of Tiger Hill

Troops of 18 Grenadiers being briefed before the attack.

Victorious troops of 8 Sikh on top of Tiger Hill after it was captured.

Soldiers of 18 Grenadiers after capturing Tiger Hill.

Soldiers of 18 Grenadiers on Tololing with weapons seized from enemy posts.

Battle of Tiger Hill

Troops of 9 Para (Special Forces) take a break after the
capture of Zulu Top.

Soldiers of 9 Para (SF) after capturing a Stinger, a man-portable
air-defence system.

Operations of 21 Para (SF)

Working their way up the treacherous mountains where the battles were fought.

Making themselves comfortable to take a break.

Getting ready to fire at the enemy.

Tololing Top and Point 4590

Soldiers of 2 Raj. Rif. occupy a firebase while attacking Tololing.

Troops of 2 Raj. Rif. after the capture of Three Pimple.

Chief of Army Staff (COAS) Gen. V.P. Malik with
the victorious troops of 2 Raj. Rif.

General Officer Commanding (GOC) Maj. Gen. Mohinder Puri,
8 Mountain Division, celebrating with the soldiers of 2 Raj. Rif.

Capt. Padmapani Acharya being promoted just before the attack on Tololing.

Triumphant soldiers of 1 Naga on the Objective.

Battle of Point 4875

13 J&K Rifles at Point 4875 after it was captured.

Capt. Vikram Batra inspecting a weapon that was seized.

Capt. Batra being pipped before the attack.

The COAS with the soldiers of 13 J&K Rifles.

Commanding Officer Col. Umesh Bawa, 17 Jat, finalizing the attack plans.

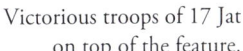

Victorious troops of 17 Jat on top of the feature.

Soldiers of 17 Jat with the weapons seized from Pakistani posts.

Capture of Point 4745

Soldiers of 1 Para (SF) get ready to attack.

Troops of 1 Para (SF) after the capture.

Soldiers of 6 Para after a successful assault.

Action of 1/3 GR

Soldiers of 1/3 GR after occupying Point 5000.

Army Aviations Corps' Role

Providing logistics support to ground troops.

Providing fire support.

Firing laser-guided bombs to destroy enemy positions.

After the War

The COAS with COs and officers.

The COAS congratulating the COs of victorious units.

Soldiers of 17 Jat with the Tricolour on Pimple 2, a part of Point 4875, after a fierce battle.

Soldiers climbing up a naked rock face.

A rocket launcher detachment of Delta Company ('D' COY) engaging a target on Tiger Hill.

Soldiers take a breather.

Troops resting at the battalion base.

Troops displaying captured weapons, ammunition and documents of the Northern Light Infantry battalion of Pakistan.

Victorious troops after capture of their objective.

The Kargil War Memorial in Dras.